**It Isn't Ugly Forever.**

By: Stacey A. Peterson

Thank you, Pete, for stumbling through
the sentence of cancer with me.
There was much more to it
than the initial diagnosis.

Thank you to my beautiful daughter, Faith.
You saved my life and made it worth living.

Thank you to the hundreds of ovarian survivors
I have met since being diagnosed.
You have shown me there are
many ways to fight this monster.

# So, What's in This Book?

*Philippians 2:3*
*Do nothing out of selfish ambition or vain conceit.*
*Rather, in humility value others above yourselves.*

This book would not have been possible without the help of so many selfless friends. They have taken the time to give back and share themselves in a very personal way so we could all grow from their time on the cancer train. I spoke with caregivers and survivors, and much of their insight became entwined through this book. I humbly attempted to put into words a *special thank you* to these beautiful people.

**Sondra:** Thank you for being a cheerleader through this process. You attended workshops and listened to guest speakers as I gathered more information and affirmation to keep writing. Sondra is my unofficial marketing specialist because every time she would introduce me or talk about my journey she would get so *"dag-gum"* excited. Sondra, your excitement is what I needed to keep writing on those hard days.

**Linda, Tony, Deann, Jacinta:** Your stories of being caregivers, whether it was as a daughter, father, or friend was inspiring because of your faith.

**Patti, Tracy:** Survivors that made this journey less lonely.

**Samir:** You entered my life as a surgeon; you offered advice like a family member and became a true friend.

**Erin and Bobbie:** The two of you were with my family from the beginning to just fill in the blanks when I couldn't see what the next step was. After all these years, your passion to help is still there, and teal runs strong through your veins.

*Colossians 3:17*
*And whatever you do, in word or in deed,*
*do everything in the name of the Lord Jesus,*
*giving thanks to God the Father through him.*

## Introduction: Creating lists

I have found it extremely important to find simple pleasures in my life. One of the most basic of these pleasures is making lists. Lists are extremely beneficial and, may I be so bold as to say, the backbone of all organization. Of course, this may just be my overanalyzing Type A personality, desperately clinging to the hope that everyone will get on board and make lists, so we can get some things done. The development of list-making is a well-orchestrated dance, an art if you will. Oh yes, I am one of *those* list makers. There is no willy-nilly list making for this girl. Some of my best lists have been color-coded, strategically made in order of importance, and creative marks were added to show delegation of the task. No one wants a dictator, so I added fun clip art and color-coding to soften the blow of my lists. I'd really like to refer to them as a "much better ways of doing things." Now, *creating the list* is fun and I will do it for the most mundane task to the most grandiose, if for no other reason than to be able to cross the item off the list and finally throw the paper away. Pure satisfaction!

Let it be known that in today's eco-friendly world I have started making lists on my phone and added a whiteboard to my office space to save on paper... *you're welcome.* Finishing a list is my way of saying *Ta-da!* to the world.

Side note: This phrase, *Ta-da!* in my opinion, should be used by more professionals than just magicians. Hairstylist, mechanics, chefs, law enforcement, and lawyers are just a few of the professions I think could pull this phrase off to the benefit of others.

Let me introduce the first caveat in this book. There are some professions that should never use *Ta-da!* If I heard *Ta-da!* from my gynecologist at any time it would be beyond awkward...*just sayin'*. As a professional, use your best judgment. Think twice before you unleash it on some unsuspecting half-naked client. Let me rephrase that. I'm not sure how many of my readers will have half-naked clients, but please know your crowd and whether you should use the phrase *Ta-da!*

I feel it is important that I say this up front. While reading this book it will feel as if you are having a conversation with me. No fancy words. No *aha!* moments. I doubt when you put this book down that you will feel inspired to run a marathon, join the monastery, or make other bold choices with your life. It's just you and me sitting on the couch with a favorite beverage.

While reading this book, however, I do hope you will feel like smiling a little. I do hope in the end you will feel I made some good points and you will be able to easily incorporate them into *your* own list to make your journey through cancer easier. Since I am a list-maker I started making a list as soon as my cancer was diagnosed. I had never gone through anything like this, so on day two I was done with my list and had no idea what to do next. I thought having a list to create order would be nice. Lists are created for everything else: preparing for a wedding, planning a birthday party, even packing for a trip. This book is my attempt to have a variety of lists for going through cancer, whether you are the patient, the caregiver, or a random bystander. Some chapters will contain mini lists, while others will be solely devoted to one beautifully orchestrated list. Some lists will be organized by dates, others may be in alphabetical order, or simply compiled to show you as the reader just how my brain is wired. *Scary, I know.*

As a caregiver, my intention is you will find some insight and feel the gratitude I share with your loved one. My goal is when you have finished reading this book you will see how making lists got me through one of the hardest times in my life. I have spent the last ten years making lists that I think will help you get through this *cray-cray* time. (See how I am trying to make this book hip for the young readers as well...*ah-haaaa*! I *am* a genius!)

The lists are scattered in among the ugliness of cancer, like wild flowers in a pasture covered with manure. The lists are there to break up the stink and the heaviness of cancer. I want the lists to keep the mood light. So, if you are limited on time you can complete a whole chapter in just minutes. I call that success in the small things!

I want you to feel empowered and educated by the lists, and on the days when the manure is just getting too deep, I want you to be able to snatch up a bouquet of my advice and advance on your journey. During my treatments, I developed an inability to focus for long periods of time. *Heck even today, I find myself losing the battle to stay focused because I am multi-tasking my day away.* Where was I? Oh yes, the lists are quick ways for me to get my point across to you so you can get the information and be on your merry way with more tools in your box.

Recently, I came across a blog that had to-do lists from Ben Franklin and Johnny Cash. Okay, I must be half-baked because even seeing other people's lists gives me such joy! I found Ben's list to be helpful because he started each day with *"What good shall I do this day?"* and ended it with *"What good have I done today?"* This is monumental! At the end of every day when you look back to see what you have accomplished, it is equally important to ask yourself how you made yourself or the world better. If we all did this, can you imagine how simply lovely the world would be? As for Johnny's list, he made some good points, but I don't think he gave it as much effort. His list included visiting his mother, kissing his wife, peeing, and not eating too much, to name a few. It just doesn't give me the same warm feeling.

> *"We pack all the madness and ambiguity of life into a structured form of writing. In short, making lists is a great way to increase our overall happiness and to feel less overwhelmed."*
> ~B.B Cooper

# Chapter 1. The Baldwin Effect or Monarchy Theory

Maybe I should start this book as if I were peeling an onion. No need for tissues just yet though. I was someone before I was diagnosed with cancer, so maybe I should start with some back story. Cue the wavy lines and harp like glissando music from a *Wayne's World* flashback...

My childhood in the rural state of South Dakota was average. Understand though, there are no complaints here. I learned how to do some amazing things growing up with parents who knew how to work hard and make a little go a long, *and I mean a long,* way. I never minded working in the garden or helping in the barn. Honestly, the best stories I tell now, besides the one you are currently reading, are from when I was a "Little Stacey." My summers were filled with softball, playing with our Brittany Spaniel, Jill, who was always older than dirt, and exploring as far as I could go on my orange bike with the crazy 'U' shaped handle bars. *Ah, the good ol' days.* Growing up on a farm offered many options for my young and creative mind. Did you know that cats will tolerate being dressed up in baby clothes, but they don't like being vacuumed?

I also learned early on that every time a frantic sibling charges at you pleading, "Don't cry!" it is most certainly the prime time to let the waterworks flow. Lastly, the sooner you learn the rule that if the tractor is running there is a good chance someone's gonna get run over, the more excitement you will experience and the longer you will live. So, if you are reading this and you grew up in the inner city, we really aren't too different. Life has handed us both some wonderful life lessons.

Our home, though the characters never changed, is made up of almost two families. There are five children in my family and the "bookends" of the family are fourteen years apart in age. I am the youngest. My perspective has always been that my parents needed to keep trying until they reached perfection; if you can believe it, there are other claims. My point of two families lies in the fact that the parents who raised my older siblings are not the same people mentally as those who raised me. The sibling closest to me in age is *five* years older. Psychologists will tell you that this gap of five years creates personality differences in the younger child. I'm not just the youngest: I also take on quirks of an only child. I find these two factors to be significant in looking at the make-up of our family.

My point is that the other four children drove my parents nuts, and I had to deal with what remained. Watching them as I went through my own health ordeal was fascinating to me, and now as a parent I cannot truly grasp how they coped. Because, as I stated before, my parents were working with about three wheels and at least one of those was flat due to the first four children driving them completely insane. We will talk later how my interesting perspective on life distracted me from my illness and simultaneously helped me to focus on how my family members were dealing with my cancer. Trust me: it was easier to get distracted than to focus on my own feelings.

As you can imagine, being the youngest of five children of parents who were too exhausted to give much of a fight certainly had its perks. Ask any of my siblings, and they will tell you how great I had it. To the contrary, I have always thought it had its drawbacks. I will admit, since my parents were worn out and physically tired from all the children and chaos the others created, I probably did get to go more places, see more things, and buy more stuff. Yet, significant setbacks came with being the last child of a large family.

I first stumbled onto my theory as a young adult, and I started to create my first hypothesis about the genetics of life. I noticed there might be an uneven distribution of the best genetic material among the five children. Please understand, I have no degree in the medical world, and I only base this phenomenon on my clairvoyance of human nature. You will see in a moment my mind-blowing discovery, and I hope you appreciate just how amazing this theory is, considering what hand I was dealt genetically. *It truly is astonishing I can tie my own shoes.*

I have named my findings the Baldwin Effect or Monarchy Theory. For centuries, the great monarchies of the world have placed the fate of their nations on the firstborn. Throughout history, even as far back as biblical times, it was the firstborn son who was given more inheritance and the role of patriarch upon his father's death. Then later in history, kings were replaced by their eldest sons after death in battle. It wasn't until the twenty-first century that the well-known monarchies of the world embraced feminism for the sake of good genetics, in my opinion, and firstborn women were to take the throne. I have to believe this scuttlebutt of promoting the firstborn was because even then the general consensus was that *good genetics will run out.* The first born will get the best genes the parents have to offer, and the more children you have the sketchier it gets. My theory is not new, and the idea can be traced to the late 1870's. I don't believe anyone ever looked at it exactly as I do, but it is good to know I am not alone in this way of thinking. It may interest you to know twenty-four of the forty-five presidents were either firstborn or the eldest sons. Twenty-one of the first 23 astronauts were the firstborn in their families *(facts.randomhistory.com/birth-order-facts.html).*

Let me be perfectly clear: I am not suggesting the firstborn children of the world are supernatural, but I do believe they got the young and sprightly genes. Look at Alec Baldwin! Later born children receive the bottom of the barrel or what I think most doctors refer to as "slim pickin's." If this isn't the case, then why would this tradition of selecting the firstborn have started and continued? Again, I feel it is important to point out that I am not a historian and these ramblings are simply from too much time on my hands, and frankly a diet of mostly sugar. I'd like to take this theory one step further, though. If two people decide to procreate and let's say they are number three and four in their own families, then we are basically working with just scraps, genetically speaking. What I'm trying to say is anything that comes forth won't be winning any Nobel Prizes, bless their hearts. For any of you who may be the youngest of a very large family, I will break it down in yet another way.

If you have ever rolled out dough for cut out cookies you know the first few batches of cookies are beautiful, flawless and perfectly shaped. Regardless of how much love and care you put into the next batches, the same thing happens every time. As you try to make the last batch, you are forced to use the leftover scraps from the cutting and forming of all those cosmetically perfect cookies. It is inevitable. In this last attempt, you will always find spots that are thinner as you roll out the dough, and you need to throw some extra bandage pieces of dough here and there so all the remaining dough can be used. *It's still a tasty cookie; don't get me wrong, it is just not going to be placed on the dessert plate for the guests.*

I can't speak for the other theorists. This was just my way of trying to understand why my body started to fall apart and none of my older siblings were feeling their years. There was only one day on my journey with cancer when the words *why me?* came out of my mouth. We are human, and we tend to want to know *why*. Toddlers are a prime example of this most basic curiosity, and when we are in a tough situation we sometimes regress. On one of those ugly days it did smack me in the face. *Why?* Why was my body in self-destruct mode? I dug into three hypotheses.

1. Geographically, all my family grew up and lived in the same area; therefore, environmental issues could not have caused my cancer.

2. Genetics: Ovarian cancer did not run in my family. Now, I have since learned that breast cancer and ovarian cancer are linked; so that must be it! That had to be why I got cancer. I have several maternal aunts and cousins who have suffered from breast cancer, all at very early ages. I had convinced myself that breast cancer would become my opponent, not something else. Before my diagnosis, I hadn't even heard of ovarian cancer. I wasn't watching for it. Years after my diagnosis, I went through genetic testing and found out I was not BRCA1 or BRACA2 positive. My cancer type was not hereditary. Strike two: there was no genetic reasoning behind my diagnosis.

3. Diet? I am not a health nut by any means, but I am not bad compared to the average Jane. I was not overweight. I didn't smoke. I'd never taken drugs. I didn't drink to excess. Why then? *Why did I get cancer?*

My theory seemed to be the answer. Simply, I was given bad genes. In my parents' drive for the perfect intellect with physical beauty, something needed to fall short. The inner workings of my genetic makeup had to be altered, you see? *Oh, the price for beauty and smarts!* As a human, I needed to find an answer, and as a smart@$$ I needed it to work in my favor. My theory did both! I had the reason why I got cancer: there had been a recall at the factory. However, knowing genetics had failed me also gave me the chance to stop searching for an answer. As we all know, when we stop looking for an answer, things seem abundantly clear. I truly believe cancer came my way to slow me down, teach me a lesson, and make my life interesting, to say the least. Ovarian cancer, as you will learn if I can convince you to read on, is the *silent killer.* The symptoms are common to most women daily, and there are no early detection tests at this time. My theory was my way of trying to make sense of everything. Upon much reflection, it's much less about theories, geographical findings, or diets and more of a God-thing than anything else.

My faith truly developed through this journey and I know that finding my cancer during pregnancy was no coincidence. I had never been one to slow down to relish a moment. God knew that. There is a great chance that had I not been so worried about the little life inside me I probably would have kept smashing full force through life. As God, would have it, cancer came at a time when it would be found, and I would be saved. That was God working in my life; I have no doubt of that.

This meant I would not be the typical statistic. Cancer came at a time when I would be helping to raise a child while fighting for my life. Maybe not the way we imagined we would raise her, but we did our best in the chaos of everything that is cancer. God was there to help us get through what seemed so impossible.

Faith didn't get baptized until she was four months old. She didn't have professional photos until she was six months old. I missed her first Halloween dressed up as a doctor because I struggled through a blood infection. This isn't the way I would have pictured life, but it worked. *God knew what He was doing.* Our daughter has no recollection of those months, and she did not suffer through any of it. As I slept through the chemotherapy treatments, she hung out in the car seat and slept through the treatments as well. She hung out with Pete at his office and chilled out like most babies do. Some say it was the worst timing for cancer, but hind sight shows me that being diagnosed with ovarian cancer while I was pregnant may have been what made me a survivor. As our daughter's hair grew in, so did mine.

Cancer became such a time-consuming process that I stopped

trying to figure out why it happened and became more focused on what to do next. *I needed a list!* I'm not the only one in our house who appreciates a good list. Pete fell into his own list making. What do we need from the store? What questions do we have for the doctors? What needs to be done around the house? The lists did not stop. The lists, our faith, and our Faith got us through cancer. The lists gave us direction. Our faith gave us power. Our new baby girl, Faith, gave us inspiration.

## Chapter 2.  I AM A SURVIVOR: Not just a *Destiny's Child* song.

*I AM A SURVIVOR.* By reading this simple sentence, you have just catapulted our relationship into about month nine. Professing *I am a survivor of Ovarian Cancer stage 1a* is something I rarely do. However, I do want to connect with you early in this story. Saying *I am a survivor* has always felt awkward to me. In my eyes, I have never fit the stereotype. I don't even bring it up in conversation, as I don't feel comfortable in the spotlight. Making that bold statement makes me feel quite vulnerable in this moment! *Quick! Tell me something private about yourself!* (What? Really? I don't believe it. Don't worry, I won't tell anyone.)

I can assume you are reading this book because:
1. you know me well and wanted to see if you are ever mentioned,
2. you, too, are a survivor or possibly a caregiver, or
3. perhaps this book has landed in your hands as a way for me to help you heal. God sends us messages all the time. And usually it isn't how we expect Him to communicate with us at all. Frequently it is not in earthquakes, but in hushed whispers.

Whatever the reason, I am thrilled you have my story. Over the last ten years, writing a book about going through ovarian cancer has crept into my mind several times. Being a survivor of ovarian cancer puts me into an exclusive group that really doesn't have a strong voice. I always wanted to be in an exclusive group, but this is not what I expected. I was thinking more of a country club or sorority. As so many mamas have said, *be careful what you wish for*. There have been enough outspoken women who have become the face of other cancers, but unfortunately word has not spread about ovarian cancer.

There are women in the public eye who are survivors of ovarian cancer; however, the average reader won't be able to name one. No worries, though. [Sound the fanfare.] I have compiled a *list* that will fix that. You will be able to see just a few of the famous ladies who battled through this particular cancer later in the book.

When I sat down to write, I began to think about why famous women haven't written their own books or starred in their own made-for-TV original dramas. They have the connections and star power, but for some reason they haven't chosen to spread the word. This is an idea that truly boggles my mind because I feel after one has made it through a journey as crazy as cancer, one needs to give back in some way. Pay it forward, ya know? It only seems logical that these well-connected women would write a book before I would.

I have a couple of hunches why these women haven't written books, been in movies, or appeared on talk shows discussing their battles. I would like to share just a couple of those possibilities with you.

One philosophy is, once an ovarian cancer patient receives her diagnosis, most do not have a favorable prognosis. You see, there is not a test to determine ovarian cancer. Pap smears do not detect ovarian cancer. Ultrasounds are only a tool in helping diagnose, but even then, it's just one of many tools that will help give a final diagnosis. Another tricky part of this cancer is the symptoms are typical and something most women will ignore. You ask any woman, on any given day, if she feels tired, bloated, has low back pain or is constipated, and she will likely say *yes*. These are some of the symptoms of ovarian cancer, but almost no woman would pay close attention to them. According to the National Ovarian Cancer Coalition website (ovarian.org), even if a woman did pay attention to these every day symptoms and actually told her doctor, there is a 66% chance she will be misdiagnosed. Most of the time doctors assume the patient is suffering from irritable bowel syndrome, acid reflux, a urinary tract infection or stress. Symptoms are easily ignored, and ineffective detection tools make this disease a silent killer. This makes it very difficult to find a candidate as a vocal spokeswoman because many of them won't survive.

My second idea of why the word is not spreading is because I believe there are many women, like myself, who don't see themselves as survivors. *Survivor* is a word I rarely use, as *I chose to not have cancer define me.* I heard that phrase somewhere, and I am choosing to agree with it. The thing is, I don't use it because aren't we all survivors of something? I was so many other things before cancer, and I have become so many things after my diagnosis. Maybe that is how others have felt and that is the reason why the general public doesn't hear as much about ovarian cancer as other cancers. The fact is that we have all gone through something major, and we need to share our journey with others. We are *thrivers* when we combine our strengths and pull through to the other side. The moments in our lives that cause us the most pain are the ones that teach us so much. We need to share that knowledge with others. That collaboration, love, and resilience is what makes us thrive. I admire your humility and modesty; however, you need to share your individual story. Your story may be what it takes to inspire someone to get up and go through another day of their struggle. It may be what finally gets another person to go in and see their doctor and not take *no* for an answer. It may save someone's life.

In the last three paragraphs, I have grown profoundly. Reflection has been good for me, and I think the reason I don't use the term *survivor* is simply, I am in denial. I don't know… I haven't watched enough talk shows to quite diagnosis myself yet. I can't be sure what makes me tick, but saying I have some denial of what I went through seems like a typical coping mechanism. The word *survivor* means cancer really happened to me. I know what you are thinking: *well duh!* The reality is as I was going through it, I usually just felt numb. I was going through the motions, from one appointment to another, but things were only sinking in on the surface. I didn't see myself as a survivor or as a cancer patient because this just couldn't really be happening to me, and denial may be why we don't hear about ovarian cancer from survivors.

Nowadays, I would say cancer crosses my conscious mind only seven percent of the time. (Seven is simply a low number and is being used to indicate I think about my past cancer experiences rarely; it has no mathematical significance.) I am finally to the point where I am not haunted by every ache or twinge. *(What was that? What does that feeling mean?)* I'm not waiting for results of some test or journaling my symptoms. I'm not looking up things on the Internet to figure out if I am undergoing normal life experiences. Life is back to what most people would see as normal. What is normal anyway?

> *"Normal is just a setting on the dryer."*
> *~Jodi Picoulet*

I had a wonderfully crazy ride on the cancer train and then I jumped off after seven consecutive weeks of chemo and numerous surgeries. I am ten years out from my diagnosis of cancer, and I still can't say the phrase "I had cancer" without choking on *that* word: *cancer*. You will usually hear me say, "When I was sick." That seems much easier to say, and give me a break, I am not technically lying. Yes, I am someone who experienced cancer first-hand and lived to tell about it. See how I didn't call myself a survivor? This seems like the perfect time to pour it all out for you. Lay it on the line and hope after reading this back story you find my story interesting enough to actually read on for the next 27 chapters.

Let us continue by quoting good ol' Charles Dickens: *"It was the best of times, it was the worst of times."* I was twenty-eight years old, and I was in my second trimester with our first child. The best of times, right? I felt amazing. I was extremely active playing softball, volleyball and golf, working, and taking last minute trips with my family. I was, for the first time in my life, really taking care of myself and avoiding all the terrible foods we are supposed to ignore. Of course, I wasn't drinking alcohol and any amount of medication I would have randomly taken for aches, pains, or allergies were also out of the picture for me. I was not chancing having any chemical in my system. I was exercising, sleeping, and eating healthy like a good pregnant lady should. As you can imagine I had read the *lists*, and I knew what to do!

The weekend before all hell broke loose I actually played in a softball game and a 27-hole best ball golf tournament. *I am woman; hear me roar!* In my naïve, conquer the world, 28-year-old mind I was awesome, and you couldn't have told me otherwise. Life was good! Nothing was going to stop me and if this was my made-for-TV moment, now is a good time to cue the music from the sitcom *Perfect Strangers*.

> Standing tall, on the wings of my dream.
> Rise and fall, on the wings of my dream.
> The rain and thunder The wind and haze
> I'm bound for better days.
> It's my life and my dream,
> **Nothing's going to stop me now.**

Then completely out of the blue at work on a Wednesday I felt "weird." Honestly that is all I can remember feeling; there was just some odd feeling in my abdomen that hadn't been there before; a tugging. I can't say it hurt; it was just "different." I called to see if I could get in to see my doctor, but I knew when your symptom was, "I'm feeling weird," I may not get too much attention. I was surprised when they had an appointment time for me that afternoon. I went in and after a quick pelvic exam I was told something felt different to them too, but I shouldn't be concerned. I was probably overdoing it, and I needed to go on bed rest. *Are you kidding me?* Buckle up, people. You are about to get a glimpse of how my mind works. I suggest you take a deep breath...

It isn't good to tell a woman who hardly sits down for commercial breaks that she needs to slow down because she knows she can empty the dryer, water the plants, and take out some meat for supper to defrost if she leaves the couch before the actors fade and the commercial jingles start. For those of you who haven't met me, here is a quick FYI: some people have described me as *high strung.*

In my head, I was convinced being on bed rest for approximately ninety days would probably make me go insane since I was still feeling pretty invincible. Grrr...I called into work and explained my situation with what could be described as incredulous mockery. The conversation went something like this. "I am so sorry. No, I'm sure it's nothing. Again, I apologize, but I can't cover the rest of my shift today. I know it will be an inconvenience for you to find help on such short notice. I am sure it's nothing, really no worries. We just want to take every precaution."

Well, bed rest lasted two days. At the end of day two at approximately ten o'clock on Friday night, I told my husband Pete, "We need to go to the hospital; something isn't right." Now, remember in Pete's mind, we had our answer. It was simple: I was overdoing it. I needed to slow down. There was no reason for me to be urging him out of bed after a long week of work. If this were a cartoon, there would be a half-naked man clinging to the ceiling light fixture saying, "What do you mean we need to go to the hospital?" He hadn't been privy to the constant urging going on in my head the past two days. I just was not content with this answer. Many women don't listen to what their bodies are saying. We are too busy and are not used to putting ourselves first. I am often asked why I went in to see the doctor, and I always feel crazy saying, "*I just felt like I needed to.*" I didn't know then that the Holy Spirit was talking to me.

Did I have symptoms? Sure. Pelvic pain, nausea, feeling tired, gaining weight, *but duh*…I was pregnant. These are all symptoms of ovarian cancer too, but all very normal signs of being pregnant; therefore, I never thought much about it. I truly believe the incessant internal push to go to the doctor that night was a spiritual connection. God was telling me to go and his plan was to have me diagnosed while I was pregnant; otherwise, I would have ignored the signs like so many women do. The dance ensued of me reassuring Pete my feelings were important enough to go to the hospital, and he needed to come off the ceiling (yet balanced with reassurance that it certainly wasn't anything for him to worry about). We just needed to be seen. Like any good expecting father would do, though he was tired, confused, and visibly shaken, Pete drove us to the hospital.

This time, after another pelvic exam, I was again told yes there was something "not right," but the nurses were unsure exactly what the problem was. I was to stay the night and in the morning, I would have an ultrasound. This sounded like a good enough plan to me. Honestly, I was just relieved I was being taken seriously instead of being on the receiving end of the sympathetic look of "you are just a new pregnant mom who is a borderline hypochondriac." I don't remember a lot about the first night in the hospital, the night before everything went upside down. I do remember there is something amazingly comforting about listening to your baby's heartbeat to let you know what you cannot see is still okay.

*Hebrews 11:1*
*Now faith is confidence in what we hope for and*
*assurance about what we do not see.*

We went down for the ultrasound the next morning. Now, for those of you who have never been in a room when a test shows something out of the ordinary, I will tell you it's an eerie, quiet, and unsettling discomfort that invades the shrinking space. WARNING: Spoiler alert! In case it isn't obvious: if you are ever in this situation, and someone gets up and leaves the room and brings more people in, it isn't a good sign. What showed up on the screen was a tumor around my left ovary. It was the size of a large grapefruit. At that moment, somewhere in my naïve and oh-so-busy world, a visual of my day calendar popped into my head, *my list for the day.* The news they were giving me didn't correlate with what my plans were for the day.

I remembered we were to attend a family picnic. I didn't have time for something to be *really* wrong. My racing out of control and multitasking life came to a screeching stop.

My lists were starting to be left undone. I was supposed to run to the store, load the car with chairs, blankets, coolers, and take the recycling to the curb. Without these items being done I felt like there was complete madness.

Sure, I wanted people to take me seriously and tell me there was merit to my feelings. I didn't want to be the crazy pregnant lady, I just didn't want anything to be seriously wrong, or heaven forbid something that would slow me down. I had things to do and things to cross off my list before my perfectly healthy baby arrived after my very normal, by-the-book pregnancy. See, I wasn't asking for much. I just wanted to have a quick-fix answer that would explain things and get me off bed rest. In my mind, the news of this mass hit me as an "inconvenience."

*I'm sorry, but we have a family picnic today. It's kind of a big deal because my parents are driving in and everyone will be meeting at the park by the zoo. You know the one. It will be great for the kids and shaded for everyone. We don't see each other often, and mom is making her potato salad. So, the medical information you are giving me right now doesn't really work for me. I appreciate your time, but, really, I need to go pick up the hot dog buns and chips. Can you hand me my clothes now?*

Needless to say, we never made it to the family picnic. The day was a little hazy. The ultrasound was scrutinized and compared to my earlier ultrasound. Whatever was growing around my ovary was as large as my baby and hadn't been there five weeks ago when I had my last ultrasound. Two not-so-good things! I remember calling my sister still thinking it would be rude not to go to the park. The least I could do would be to call and have her get the chips. In a lighthearted somewhat rushed sing-songy voice I remember saying:

"They found a mass. They aren't sure what it is, maybe a cyst, maybe cancer. So, um we can't make it to the park today. Please let everyone know for us. Have a good time and we will catch up with you later…Okay?"

Not sure if I said it that way for her benefit or mine. *La-la-la*, no big deal. Let me take just a moment to address some things. First of all, any doctors who have happened upon this book, here is my first piece of advice to you. Please don't ever tell someone the broadest spectrum of the situation: It could be nothing or it could be death. *Really?* Even I, a simple amateur, could make *that* conclusion. It does no one any good to make this chasm of a declaration. Secondly, if this comment is supposed to make the patient think, "It must be the first scenario: I have excellent luck!" then you are wrong again.

Human nature always makes us think it must be death. Covering all the possible answers doesn't reassure anyone, and frankly it makes you look like an idiot. Okay, enough said.

I do remember one more thing from that whirlwind day. Of course, after the shock of the ultrasound, more diagnostic testing needed to be done. Somehow when you enter the doors of a hospital, you enter a vortex of time that exists in no other arena. In a hospital, time seems to move so slowly you find yourself wondering if you have been sitting in this gown five minutes or five hours. At other times, you can actually see people moving around quickly, but you are not able to hear what is happening until you are suddenly shocked back into reality by a metal tool crashing to the floor or the hand of a stranger on your forearm. That morning someone had pushed the fast-forward button. I was suddenly being taken to the bowels of the hospital for an MRI. I was being told so many things and none of it was making sense. I was seeing back hallways and elevators of the hospital, an experience saved for very few people.

*Go, go, go.*

I heaved myself out of the wheel chair, waddled over to the machine, and finagled myself onto the sliding table that would bring me into the depths of this monster. My mind was racing and my eyes seemed to be playing their own game of pinball. If you have never been slid into a MRI machine, I think it would be comparable to the first few minutes of being buried alive. The extremely small space they ease you into is confining and utterly miserable. The smooth confinement is inches from your face, and the magnet whirling around your body is loud. My heart was racing and my breath erratic. Then suddenly I was conscious of my surroundings. Wait…a familiar sound seeped into the coffin-like space. I became gratefully aware they had piped in music as a way of distracting me from my possible claustrophobia.

That song…. I knew that song.

A wide smile crossed my face. I think a small giggle escaped me. Anyone watching probably thought I had gone insane. It is at that moment my mind figured out how to deal with what was ahead: distraction.

> *"And like a little girl cries in the face of a monster that lives in her dreams* **Is there anyone out there 'cause it's getting harder and harder to breathe."**

Ah, Maroon 5. I don't know why, but these words were the comedy relief I needed. As I was sandwiched in this humming machine that felt like it was swallowing me, the unknown was certainly a monster from a dream to this girl! The words just seemed to fit. I felt alone and scared and the stress level had increased to dramatic levels. Those words made me laugh and stop holding my breath. It seems odd, but the song brought me out of this fast-forward-spinning, out-of-control state, and it set a mood that helped me to tackle cancer. I started to deal with all the chaos by finding humor in all of it and watching the other people around me rather than focusing on myself. During this distraction, the MRI ended and I returned to my room where the waiting began. This, dear reader, was "the worst of times." Or so I thought. *Stay tuned for the twist.*

Doctors, nurses, and hospitals in general don't run on any kind of time that correlates to the outside world. If you have ever been inside a hospital, you know what I mean by this. The phrase, "The doctor will be in to talk over options with you," does not even mean the doctor is in the building at the time this phrase is uttered. It means on some day ending with $y$ (and could either be odd or even), "a" doctor will probably mistakenly step into *your* room thinking it was the lounge. Hours passed. I mean a full day of hours passed and then finally a surgeon, to whom I will refer from this point on as the Spawn of Satan, came in to speak with me. She had taken so long to find my room that she stepped in just after Pete stepped out to grab something to eat, wash up, and feel more human. Of course, this is just the way life works. She was completely competent. In fact, I found out she was the best OB/GYN oncologist at this particular hospital. While all of that may have been true, she didn't listen and could not wrap her mind around the fact this young mother, who she found alone with her thoughts, was scared. *Beyond scared.* You see, the world is funny sometimes. The moments of the last twelve hours were at that moment finally catching up with me.

Tumor.
The dimensions.
Possible cancer.
Emergency surgery.

They had all caught up and had just crashed into the back of my eye sockets. These are the thoughts racing through my head when this woman appeared in my room.

But wait! It gets better because the Spawn of Satan, this surgeon, who had landed in my room, possibly due to poor navigational skills, had been in the local newspaper that very day. No lie. She was explaining her thoughts on when a baby is truly a baby. Interesting concept that I won't tackle in this book, but this is what she said…26 weeks. On the day of my first surgery, I was going to be exactly 26 weeks along. Minutes before she entered my room I had been asking myself this question: was exactly 26 weeks less important than 26 weeks and one day, or 26 weeks and five days pregnant? I remember telling this woman, who wasn't even making eye contact with me that the goal needed to be for *both* my baby and I to get through this surgery. Saving just me shouldn't be the end result. Let's say she was indignant, because what I want to say probably cannot be printed. This woman was cutting into me in twelve hours, and I was not reassured by her skill that I would still be pregnant when I woke up. To say I was timorous, discouraged, petrified, or disheartened, (thank you thesaurus.com for this lovely list) is an understatement.

This woman's bedside manner was less than ideal. She in no way put me at ease and if I hadn't been determined to stay at that hospital for delivery I would have gathered up my gown in the back and shuffled right out of there. She was a wonderfully skilled surgeon, but not the intellectual support I needed. Because of her demeanor she received the vile nickname of Satan's Spawn. You will see that our journey together, though short lived, was full of venom and destruction.

This woman nodded at me and halfheartedly listened to my fears and comments. She left me alone again to stew on life and what would come. I held my swollen belly and listened to my little one's heartbeat. The beat was strong, steady, and so reassuring. I felt guilty I was bringing my little one through this, yet *oh* so glad there was someone whispering to me, "All is okay, and we are in this together."

I need to backtrack for a minute. It's important to know this was not exactly the first time this mass was found. When I started to write this story, I asked for my medical records to be sent to me to get the facts straight and make sure I was giving details that created a complete picture. Imagine my surprise when I came across the records of my very first visit to the emergency room in early 2006. This is where Faith's journey really started. After five days of lower abdominal pain, pain that kept me from standing up straight and pain that was only curbed by lying in the fetal position, I drove myself to the after-hours clinic. I was sure I must have a hernia, appendicitis, or Crohn's disease. It's amazing what five days curled up in a ball will do to your rational thinking process.

Looking back at the records, it is interesting to see the twists and turns my story took even before I knew it was being written. We had been on fertility medication for only a month, and I was sure pregnancy did not look like this. Women complained about feeling sick or tired, but I had never heard of someone wanting to be put down by a dart gun to make the pain stop. When I went to the clinic and they wanted to do a pregnancy test, I thought they were crazy. At that point, though, I really didn't care what they wanted me to do; I just wanted the pain to stop because I had things to do! The only time I was ever told I was going to be a mom was from some unhappy weekend doctor who told me, and then instantly said, "You are either going to the emergency room in an ambulance or you need to find a ride immediately because we think your pain is from an ectopic pregnancy." Ectopic pregnancies, also called tubal pregnancies, happen in about one of every fifty pregnancies, and it simply means the fertilized egg stays in your fallopian tube instead of traveling to your uterus.

I called a friend, and she hung out with me until Pete could get back into town. I remember being in a bit of a daze and watching Super Bowl XL where the Seattle Seahawks lost to the Pittsburg Steelers. It was at this point in our lives that Pete started using the phrase "You have the worst timing ever." Why did I have to be in the hospital while the Super Bowl was on?

You see we are a big sports family. Subscribing to the extra sports channels is a no brainer. Unfortunately for Pete, from that day forward I have subconsciously turned the channel during extra innings, started a deep conversation when I needed his full attention in the last two minutes of a game while our team was in the red zone, or demanded the TV was too loud for me to sleep even though it was during game seven of the NBA playoffs. These have all actually happened. I love sports; I really do. They just started becoming less important to me after that day.

During the exam at urgent care we had an ultrasound, and an ectopic pregnancy was not completely ruled out. I did stay overnight for observation and was discharged the next day. When I read back over the medical records from that night in the ER, my novice eyes do fall upon some interesting material. Even ten years later, I feel it is important to look deeper into what was being said and to have a doctor make sense of the notes. This is what I found in my medical notes from the medical staff the February night:

> *Therefore, the emergency room ordered an ultrasound which showed an ovarian cyst and a mass behind the uterus, probable solid mass, consistent with a fibroid.*

In the following day's records, the nurse states:

> *In the right adnexa there appears to be a prominent irregular cyst involving the right ovary. Right ovary itself measures 4.2 x 3.5 cm. Posterior to the right ovary there is a partially cystic and partially solid mass measuring 6.1 x 5.7 cm. Posterior to the uterus there is a large solid mass with blood flow measuring approximately 5 x 7cm. Just adjacent to this very large mass there is what is believed to be the left ovary; however, there are no follicles in this area and the findings measure 2.9 x 2.7 cm. There is a small amount of free fluid in the pelvis. There is no intrauterine pregnancy identified.*

I find it interesting that under the column "impression" in the notes it is restated:

> *There is a cyst that is partially solid and is to the right of this larger mass. The left ovary appears solid and somewhat unusual in appearance and the right ovary contains a large cyst.*

The findings were called into the Department of Emergency Medicine. Those notes read as follows:

*Findings are nonspecific; however, ectopic pregnancy is
not ruled out and would be somewhat of a concern.
Findings do not have typical appearance of dermoid or
teratoma and other ovarian masses are certainly
possible.*

Nothing was ever done with this mass. The pain subsided, and
no mention of this incident was brought up. Since there was no
follow-up or concern about this mass, I can't help but wonder if
it was a fibroid or if it was the beginning of the tumor that
would soon encompass my left ovary. Hindsight of course is
20/20. As I started to unravel these details for this book, I called
my dear friend and the man who saved my life, Dr. Samir. I
began to ask him questions about these findings that happened
before he ever entered my made-for-TV drama.

He started the conversation with his thick Middle Eastern accent
and the words *"Stacey, Honey,"* which of course made me
smile from ear to ear. His tone transported me to his home
office filled with books and family items. His teddy bear
warmth could be felt over the telephone and immediately gave
me comfort. It had been so long since I had talked to him. I had
forgotten how soft spoken and caring he was. He dispensed this
fatherly advice in a soft tone and he reassured me, "What they
found was probably the early forming of the tumor that would
eventually be identified and removed. At that particular time, it
would have been odd and not typical medical practice to search
more into what they thought was a fibroid. You were pregnant,
and searching further into speculation would not have been safe
for the baby." He has always known what to say and when to
say it.

On a TV show, I once heard that new doctors tend to see hoof
prints and think they were made by a zebra instead of a horse. I
think the analogy works well here. The mass *was* seen as a
horse by veteran doctors instead of a zebra. In my odd case, it

really was a zebra that made those tracks...*who knew?*

## Chapter 3. Surgery...

Just four days after my first feelings of *something being weird,* I was prepped for surgery. I had to laugh as I read through the records and saw the assessment notes from the nurse.

> *"Assessment completed. Patient complains of being very tired. **'This is all hard to take in.'** Patient encouraged that the baby has looked good on monitor, moving etc."*

I found this statement comical because my emotions seemed practical, and I was surprised they were noteworthy. However, I also found it reassuring as I read through a lot of the medical measurements and jargon of my notes, that the nurses included simple statements about me. The notes became very human when instead of measurements there was a reflection or specific comments from me. On any given day nurses see dozens of patients. I would imagine it becomes a blur to them. It seems more likely that terms like *the cranky lady in room fifty-three, the snorer in room eighteen,* or *the old codger down the hall,* would be written in hospital notes rather than the wandering thoughts a patient was having. I can tell you from experience, and you can see from some moments already shared in this book, hospitals are a business. Not all hospital staff will see you as a person nor, will they see beyond your health matter. Sometimes it will be more like standing in line at the customer service desk for twenty minutes to be told, "I'm sorry I can't help you right now it's time for my break." Most of the time I found myself lucky when it came to hospital staff and have found a quote that explains nurses well.

*"Not all angels have wings, some wear scrubs."*

The morning of the surgery, July 16, was a blur. It had been decided that I would be prepped for abdominal surgery to remove the tumor. Anything growing that fast needed to be removed and biopsied right away. The first idea was to remove the mass laparoscopically. This would mean a small incision in the wrinkle of my bellybutton and the mass being removed through another small incision and tube. Unfortunately, plan B was required. The mass was too large to exit my body through a tube; a large incision would be created down my abdomen. I was never given any percentages of our baby's survival but, I certainly wasn't given high hopes either. Going into surgery was one of life's unknowns where you let go and let God.

I remember saying to my husband of then five years, *"When I wake up from surgery don't be annoying! Don't do that stupid thing you always do of asking a million questions. I don't want to reach over and poke your eye out, but I will. Pete, I know you think it is a way of having a conversation but no, it really isn't."*

He is a smart man and agreed to comply. I was wheeled down a hallway to a cold room, and the nurse handed Pete a machine that looked a lot like what you get at restaurants to alert you when your table is ready. You know the small, square, black device that lights up and vibrates? This was the one-sided communication device Pete clung to so he could get signals of what was happening during surgery. The instructions went something like this. The first buzz indicated surgery had started. The next buzz three hours later indicated the end of surgery. The last buzz meant he needed to pick up the phone in the lobby to connect with the nurse for further instructions, or his table was ready and the nurse would be telling him the daily specials. It was something to that effect.

If this were a television show, this is where there is a close-up of the tears streaming down my face. Pete was holding my hand and whispering he loved me, and he told me he would be right there when I returned from surgery. The gurney was slowly pushed down the hall and finally we were too far apart and our physical tie to one another was severed. It suddenly got real. I had to smirk when I read through the medical notes later; they described my emotional behavior at that moment as *"apprehensive crying."* What does anyone expect at that point from the patient? I'm just thrilled *that* was all I was doing!

I remember waking from surgery and instantly and instinctively reaching for my stomach, a sign I was already a mom, regardless of whether people wanted to believe I was carrying a real person.

The nurse in the post-op was right there speaking to me in her trained "comforting voice." She asked me how I was doing. I ignored her and asked, "How is my baby?" Reassurance came immediately and was then strangely followed instantly with the overwhelming feeling of pain. No, seriously, *a lot of pain.* The nurse tried to be calming to no avail. She sounded the retreat horn and asked if I wanted her to call Pete down to the post-op room. In my slightly drugged stupor I said "yes," but he could only come down if he would not ask stupid questions. Please don't hold this comment against me. I was drugged, but obviously not effectively drugged hence the excruciating pain. Because of my excruciating pain my eyes were closed and I couldn't see the nurse's face. I experienced the slightest amount of entertainment as I heard her call Pete in the waiting room with those exact demands. "You can come, but she said you can't ask any stupid questions."

Ah, comedy relief.

Also during this phone call, the nurse informed Pete they had given me a lot of medication, enough that I really shouldn't have even been conscious, let alone in any kind of pain.

It wasn't long before Pete was down in the post-op room with me. He didn't ask stupid questions, but the pain didn't stop either. I stayed in this uncomfortable physical and emotional state for two and half hours. I didn't realize how much time had passed until I looked at the medical records years later. I blame this on the time vortex theory. Now looking back through the notes, the nurse was giving the surgeon and pain management doctor updates every thirty minutes. I never stated I was lower than a ten on the pain scale. The nurse's notes include at 13:10 (1:10pm) "patient having large amounts of pain," and an hour later "patient continues to have a lot of pain," and still later in the evening at 17:15 (5:15pm) "notified dr. the patient has pain after hour lockout dose met."

The doctor and the anesthesiologist came in at 15:50 (3:50 pm) or approximately three hours after they moved me to the recovery room. The two doctors chatted over me reassuring each other they did not leave "things" inside me. (Well, thank goodness that wasn't the case! I would hate to think my writhing in pain for hours was a result of the inability to accurately count how many clamps had been removed.)

Then they moved on to talking about drugs. Not to me, mind you, but still over me and to each other. What kind was I given? How much? It was then that Satan's Spawn decided to look at me, and I was notified I shouldn't be in any pain. Well, okay then, if I shouldn't be in any pain, I'll just stop writhing. *My bad!* She wasn't used to things not going as she planned, and I was becoming an inconvenience. Again, I want to take this time to talk to any medical personnel. My advice to you is *don't be dumb*. That is a rookie mistake and it really is beneath you. Telling me I shouldn't be in pain is obviously not sound medical advice.

More wonderful meds were given and my goal of not taking chemicals while pregnant was completely annihilated. Forgive me for jumping to the next day, but honestly there may have been monkeys in my room doing the *cha-cha* and I wouldn't have remembered it. (Now that would sell some books. Yes, yes, there were *definitely* monkeys doing the *cha-cha* in my room, and they were dressed in rainbow tutus. Western medicine: *gotta love it!*

In the medical records, I find this as the description from the surgery.

> *"The specimen is submitted in two parts, part one is labeled 'left tube and ovary' and consists of a 567-gram left ovary with tube measuring 13.0x 5.0 x 12.0 x 8.0cm. A short segment of fallopian tube measuring 3.0cm is noted. The fallopian tube is pink and a fine fimbriated edge. The serosal surface of the mass is tan-pink, glistening, with a prominent vasculature. The mass is well encapsulated. On cut section, the largest nodule is tan-pink and 9.0 cm in diameter. Next to the large area is a hairy area of yellow-pink nodular material measuring 5.0 x 5.0 cm. This area contains a moderate amount of white sebaceous-like material."*

Pardon me if you have eaten recently, that description is a lot to process. This description is common for a teratoma that may contain several different types of tissue and sometimes mature elements such as hair, muscle, teeth, and bone. I wish there was a picture because what I imagine is horrific looking.

There were still so many unknowns. This surgery was just the beginning. At this time, the tumor that was removed and my unborn baby were approximately the same size. It is no wonder now that the rudest people had been asking this newbie mom if I were carrying twins. *No, just a tumor. Thanks.*

Recovery was typical after the initial pain "incident" was resolved. However, to this day the one thing that is still incredibly hard for me is the ten-inch scar that travels downward from just under my rib cage, makes a crazy detour around my navel and then continues to go down, down, down. Scars are nature's way of always reminding us of the lessons we have had in life. Some lessons are more fun to remember than others, like the time you played softball all summer and kept ripping up the same spot on your leg from sliding. Wow, you were a monster to be reckoned with. Lesson #15: You were once invincible. Then there are the scars your five-year-old can't stop staring at. She reaches out to trace it and you quickly turn away feeling self-conscious. Her interest is innocent and she just wants to know what happened. In retelling an age appropriate version of the story, you start to tear up. This scar has you wishing you would never have to tell your child about anything bad in life...*ever*. Lesson #35: *You are no longer invincible.* Ten years after this scar was made, the details of this bumpy detour in my life have faded. The scar, however, does not fade.

Though it is typically ignored in my fast-paced life, there are times it can still transport me to the first time I saw it. The moment when I looked down and thought, *"I am Frankenstein. I am not beautiful. I will never be the same."* It took me a long time to understand life isn't ugly forever. More scars will come in this adventure. Both physical and emotional, but please read on to hear the rest of my story and, more importantly, *you need the lists!*

> *"Never be ashamed of a scar. It means you were stronger than whatever tried to hurt you."*
> ~Author Unknown

# Chapter 4. As promised: Just some of the ladies that are in the club.

Here are just some of the wonderful ladies you may have heard of who have battled ovarian cancer:

1. Carol Channing * surviving. She is known for her raspy voice and singing/acting career. She debuted in 1949 with *Gentlemen Prefer Blondes* and *Hello, Dolly.*

2. Kathy Bates * surviving. Kathy Bates is best known for her acting roles in *Misery* and *Fried Green Tomatoes.* I recently saw her on Stand Up to Cancer.

3. Coretta Scott King died at 78 from ovarian cancer according to The Atlanta Journal-Constitution. She was an American author, activist, and civil-rights leader, and the wife of Martin Luther King, Jr.

4. Gilda Radner died at 42. Gilda entertained us on Saturday Night Live with memorable characters like Roseanne Rosannadanna and her personal parody of Barbara Walters.

5. Jessica Tandy died at 85. I am sure you remember her from her roles in *Cocoon* and *Driving Miss Daisy.*

6. Ann Dunham died at 52, the mother of U.S. President Barack Obama.

7. Shannon Miller * surviving. According to encyclopedia.com she is still the most decorated American gymnast.

8. Barbara Parks passed away at 66 while I was writing this book. She is known in every elementary school for writing the *Junie B. Jones* children series.

9. Diem Brown passed away at the age of 34 years while I was writing this book. I had the privilege of meeting this *Real-World Reality TV* star in 2014.

10. Dinah Shore died at 78. An American singer, actress, television personality, and the top-charting female vocalist of the 1940s according to biography.com.

11. Tracy Carmon joined the Lord at age 43. A dear friend who taught me how to embrace life and give glory to God.

12. Hope Aguilar * surviving and thriving. She has helped me stay motivated to write down my own story. Check out her book *HOPE.*

13. Patti Emerson * who loves being a grandma and continues to give me wonderful ideas. For instance, ordering coffee with a British accent just to shake things up, or for entertainment purposes. We all need to laugh more.

14. Keva Jackson, was a strong and beautiful woman who never let ovarian crack her pristine exterior.

15. Debby Miller, * who has made it her passion to spread the word on genetic testing. Please visit her website at www.ovariancancertrials.org/

16. Madonna Kilcollum, * who decided that women needed to be given the right comfort items and educational materials upon diagnosis. She has helped the National Ovarian Cancer Coalition distribute tens of thousands of kits to women.

The last six women on this list are famous in my world. These were beautiful people who were hazed into this elite group like I was. It's the not so famous people that survivors lean on and gain so much hope from because we are in the trenches with them at meetings, in treatments and through community celebrations. We are shoved into the spotlight and a microphone is thrust into our hands. We are now the spokeswomen for this disease. No training, no understudy. Us: every moment. But it isn't a one woman show. There is hope and women are winning. We are making a difference and we are making teal known!

"I got all my sisters with me!" Sister Sledge

## Chapter 5. Getting Ornery

*You aren't yourself when you are hungry...*
I found this candy bar and felt like I had won the lottery.

This was made for me!

Cancer was a large ugly pothole in the road of life for me. It was scary, but I wouldn't say unfortunate. I know you think I am crazy, but please hear me out. Being told I had cancer at 28 changed me into someone I may have never become, or at least, people who really know me can say I wouldn't have become any time soon. I have explained it like this: I can be a little slow at times. (Baldwin Theory at work again.) To get my attention I really needed a gong next to my ear to get me to focus on a different direction, and cancer did that. I was powering forward like a locomotive, never taking a deep breath or long looks at the grass swaying in the wind. I was 28, after all.

Cancer brought clarification for me. It has also brought out some orneriness only 90-year-olds should have. Please don't hold that against me. If you are going to get through your own diagnosis my advice is you will need at least 17.23% orneriness. Caveat number two; this percentage has no scientific basis at all, and there will be times when it's more like 22%. I read a meme recently about people having an inner child. The meme said, "I have an inner old lady who says inappropriate things, tells everyone to be quiet, and wants to go to bed at 8pm." That's me!

Being ornery is in my blood. If you have met any of my family, you could honestly say, "She comes by it naturally." No lie, Granny Elizabeth used to poke people with a stickpin, in church, if they were sitting in *her* spot. I mean really! Who even thinks of doing that, and if the thought did cross your mind, would you honestly try it in church of all places? I am sure she had some explaining to do to Ol' St. Peter! This is what I mean by orneriness!

This ornery gene was passed down to my dad. Now before you read on, please understand 1) genetics are strong, 2) my father grew up in a rural state in the 1950's, and 3) the threat of PETA coming to stop him never came to fruition. The story goes that he would wrangle bull snakes from the tall prairie grasses and shove them into mailboxes. He loved hiding close by to watch his cousins, aunt, and even the innocent mail carrier *open* the mailbox. Seeing the chaos that ensued when the reptile was discovered makes him chuckle to this day. Needless to say, there were many days the mail was not delivered.

That is orneriness defined.

I can say it did not skip me, and my daughter is also loaded with it. Years after my cancer diagnosis, I received a personal message on Facebook referencing one of my cancer posts. It was from a guy I used to go to high school with; we maybe had one class together and I hadn't heard from him in 20 years. He said something about cancer meeting its match and he would bet on me every time. That really got me thinking. First of all, what did I do to this guy in high school? Seriously, what kind of badass persona had I been emitting in my teens? Because honestly, I thought my Mary Catherine Gallagher impression of a mild-mannered student who inevitably does something loud and inappropriate was how everyone saw me. Secondly, thank you for thinking I could win this fight. I guess Granny's genes were laying a little closer to the surface than I thought. It amazes me how we walk through our days thinking we are projecting one image and then find out later we had people thinking something completely different. What an eye-opening moment. I think it would be extremely helpful to be able to see ourselves from someone else's perspective sometimes.

I'm about to tell you something you already know, but needs to be said: this journey is going to be ugly. It will be like no other storm you have endured, but I want you to know and believe; you've got this! Looking out from your hospital bed is giving you a different perspective than what I see. You are going to be strong and beautiful while blowing this cancer thing out of the water! There is support out there for you, and a positive attitude will get you through most of this hellish ordeal. Have faith that your doctors know how to help you. Believe in yourself! You can make it through treatment, and, remember, you don't have to do any of this on your own.

When you start to have doubt, get ornery! The best example of my aforementioned advice as to why you need to get ornery is that during this long and tiring journey you will need to be your own advocate. You will need the orneriness of Granny to get you what is needed, wanted, and deserved. This ornery attitude first came for me in the diagnosis process. I needed to be heard. I was not a number, and waiting was not something I was going to tolerate.

I am not the only one who feels that this is a major part of the fight. Being your own advocate means you will need to speak up and really be heard by medical staff and caregivers. Up to this point in the book you may think that I was not only fighting for my life, but I was fighting against the medical personnel I encountered. Well, that's kind of true. You will need to read on to hear about the superhero who swoops in. Yes, every story needs one and mine is like no other (picture Dom DeLuise with a Middle Eastern accent). I don't want to give too much away at this point, but this man, who I now call a friend, dedicated his professional life to saving women and making their lives better. Even at this point in his retirement he still travels to foreign countries to help women who would surely die from the lack of good medical help. He, of course, saves women with skilled hands and a brilliant mind, but more than that, he saves women using his big heart. He does all this while keeping the cape tucked under his lab coat. I'm getting ahead of myself though. Dr. Samir Abu Ghazaleh agreed to go on this crazy ride with me to save my life, and he continues this crazy ride as I try to reach more families with this book.

He will share the next list with you of how to talk to doctors so they will listen. It can be extremely frustrating when you say one thing and everyone hears you say something else and you don't get the quality of care you need. Dr. Samir, after thirty-three years of practice, has been able to lay out a list of tips that will help you communicate with your doctor. This man is a true gift from God, and I would literally do whatever he says. It may have something to do with the fact when everyone else's doctor was telling them to only eat fruits and veggies; Dr. Samir told me I could eat chocolate cake and drink wine. In my world, the man made a lot of sense!

Another reason Dr. Samir is beyond phenomenal is when I asked for his help in making a book of lists that would help ovarian cancer patients and caregivers, he gave me lists within lists. He knows what I like! Here are a few ideas from a doctor of what to do to beat this disease. Much of this information is specific to ovarian cancer, but the general idea can be applied with almost any health scare. Dr. Samir and I worked together to compile this list, and it is clear where the science stops and my ramblings are interjected.
Dr. Samir's list:
> 1. The Internet: Friend or Foe... If you go to the
> Internet, go to a reputable, accurate site:

A. National Cancer Institute (NCI)
   www.cancer.gov

B. American Cancer Society (ACS)
   www.cancer.org

C. Society of Gynecologic Oncologists (SGO)
   www.sgo.org

D. American College Obstetrics/Gynecology
   (ACOG) www.acog.org

E. American College of Surgeons (ACoS)
   www.facs.org

You may want to visit the Internet after the first consultation with your physician, as you will have some specifics for which you would like more information. While you are on the web, check the doctor's specialty. Is he or she specialized in your type of cancer? This is very important! For example, if you have cancer of the ovary, you will need a gynecologic oncologist. If you have breast cancer, you will need a medical oncologist, breast surgeon or at least a general surgeon. Being a licensed MD does not mean he or she specializes in your type of cancer. Often a website will say a doctor has an interest in a certain disease; however, this does not mean the doctor is specialized or board certified in that specialty. Unfortunately, some doctors think they are capable of caring for patients beyond their expertise.

2. I know you are trying to be helpful, but don't…

A. Be careful of personal testimonies. Many of these are not scientific and may not be accurate.

B. Also hearing about your dog walker's neighbor's sister's cousin's mother who had this bump that wouldn't go away will not do you any good.

3. Doctors and Hospitals are not created equally...
   A. When you start your research be sure to include the doctors, hospitals, and the institution where you will be receiving the treatment as well.

   B. Be prepared to meet with your doctor. If you weren't able to find the information you needed on your specific doctor, then have a short list of questions.
      a. Are they specialized, and board certified in this type of cancer?

      b. If not, whom can they recommend?

      c. If your doctor wants to refer you to a specialist, be careful of internal (institution, clinic) referral, unless they fulfill the above criteria. There are some doctors who will only recommend a coworker instead of what is best for you.

To be treated by a qualified, specialized doctor at a qualified specialized institution is crucial.

4. "Attention all personnel, choppers on the upper and lower pads. Both shifts report for surgery." (Who doesn't love M*A*S*H?)
   A. Be prepared for your first consultation.
      a. Take a relative or a friend with you. Detailed and foreign information will be dumped upon you and the longer

you are in the room and the more information you get, the harder it will be to retain the information correctly. You will need another set of ears and eyes.

   b. Write down a list of questions. Don't make the questions too long, and know that no question is stupid; you are most likely not a medical professional. Talk to the doctor face-to-face and try to concentrate on what they tell you. Finally, before moving onto the next question, jot down some notes to remind yourself of the conversation. Between your notes, focused conversation and the insights from the third party you brought with you to the visit, you should have a great resource to rely on.

B. Dr. Samir helps in making your list to talk to your doctor:

   a. Since you are a cancer specialist, have you seen patients with my type of cancer?

   b. With treatment, what is the outcome?

   c. If things don't go well, will I suffer?

   d. Will I lose my hair? What will happen with my sexual life? etc.

A great deal of your questions during subsequent visits will focus on side effects of treatment and their management. This can be addressed, by the nurse, oncology nurse, or nurse practitioner who works within the medical group. These nurses often can go into more depth about side effects, adverse effects, and treatments for nausea, dry mouth, etc.

    C. If you notice your doctor comes to talk to you while standing or with his or her hand on the door knob, ask your doctor politely, "I know you are very busy, but would you please sit down? I have questions and I need some answers."

Dr. Samir retells this specific story that I think many patients can understand. "One Saturday morning, while making my rounds, a patient and I were joking and laughing. As I was leaving the room, a lady patient from across the hall was standing at her door with tears in her eyes. I asked her, 'what seems to be the problem?' She indicated that it was me. 'I did not mean to eavesdrop, but I feel jealous. Here you are talking and laughing with your patient, and I can never talk to my own doctor as he usually zips in and out of my room like lightning.' I told her when her doctor comes to make rounds later in the day, before he leaves, ask him politely if he would sit down, because you have questions and you need answers. When he does, pull out your list of questions. The next day she was waiting at her door for me, to tell me her doctor was very apologetic. "He sat down for a long time, answering all my questions."

This empowerment is how all patients should feel.

More from Dr. Samir:
I made it a habit in my practice to say to the patients at the end of the first consultation: If and when things go well, we will rejoice together. However, if they do not, I promise you:
    1. I will not neglect you as long as I am your doctor.
    2. I will not let you suffer under my watch.
    3. I will not give you any treatment, unless it has a potential of benefiting you.

Don't be shy to ask the business office or patient navigator about financial aid. An initial meeting can usually be set up just by notifying the nurse you are interested in speaking with the patient navigator. In my experience, the nurse reached out directly to staff for me and the patient navigator visited me in my room. Talking with a business manager is helpful if you do not have insurance or your insurance is inadequate. This is not mandatory (as this is *not* your responsibility) and will be handled by the doctors and hospital staff if you choose to do nothing. Your biggest job is to know what your insurance plan covers.

Payment plans can be set up and talking with a hospital employee about financial plans that are offered may reduce your stress over this situation. When the business manager calls to tell you the amount, understand that the first payment plan they present is not your only option. Tell them what amount you can pay each month. There are many resources in the hospital offices that can be used to assist you, and by simply talking with the patient navigator the help will come to you. I would tackle this assignment much like the initial appointment with your doctor. Make a list and remember to ask whatever is on your mind. It is better to have the information than to make mistakes because you didn't know what your options were.

Talking with a patient navigator can help you find out what you don't know. Patient navigators will be able to assist you in finding transportation to and from appointments, support groups, financial assistance, ways to cope with depression and stress, and understanding disability and social security benefits. These angels are there to help you tackle concerns with your health care team or with your children, family, friends, or co-workers. They have the resources to help patients understand how cancer impacts intimacy and identity issues. They are there to help you go beyond the cancer diagnosis, all at no cost to you.

*"Always remember, you are the patient. All of the doctors, nurses, hospital chiefs, and personnel are meant to work for you."*
~Dr. Samir

Now, can you see why I like the guy so much?

Unfortunately, there is a good chance ovarian cancer patients will be misdiagnosed. They will need to be ornery and be equipped to be their own advocates. Many times, what women explain to the doctor is not what the doctor hears. There is the chance that they are going to be told they suffer from what the last fifteen patients had because the symptoms are similar. You may hear doctors say, "It is that time of year; it must be a virus." There *is* a chance hypochondriacs were in their office all morning and it's only human for the doctor to assume what you are saying has to do with the latest craze created by the television doctor or some medical website. A survey organized by the National Ovarian Cancer Coalition reported more than two-thirds of the women polled were initially misdiagnosed with ovarian cancer by their doctors. I feel that the chances of being misdiagnosed are extremely high and this is due to the fact there are no diagnostic tests for this disease. However, breast cancer, which has tests to accurately diagnose the disease, has 10,000 cases per year that are misdiagnosed. Some reports show breast tissue biopsies are incorrect a third of the time, leaving close to fifty thousand misdiagnosed, this from an article by Dr. Joann Elmore and Dr. David Rimm published in the Journal of the American Medical Association (JAMA). Please note these results have been questioned by JAMA.

I still say you know your body better than anyone else. You need to listen to the little voice in your head that says, *Go see your doctor. Get a second opinion. No, I think it is something else.* For me, it was the constant voice telling me, *I feel weird; something isn't right.* Hey, if we listen to that voice when it tells us to buy the clearance dress or eat the last piece of pizza, then shouldn't we listen when it is something as important as our health? Invite the Holy Spirit to lead your decisions and emotions today.

> Dear God,
> I pray that the Holy Spirit will *teach* me,
> Your wisdom will *guide* me,
> And your love will *move* me.
> Amen.

By inviting the Holy Spirit into your life, you are making the strongest cancer fighting team available. The Holy Spirit is different from having God on your side or praying specifically to Jesus. By asking the Holy Spirit to lead your decisions and guide your actions you are employing the same power Jesus used to raise the dead and heal lepers. The Holy Spirit helps power us forward and allows us to hear his healing words and see the strength around us and within us. You will need the Holy Spirit as you fight for yourself.

*Romans 8: 26-27*
*The Spirit helps us in our weakness. We do not know what we ought to pray for, but the Spirit himself intercedes for us through wordless groans. And he who searches our hearts knows the mind of the Spirit, because the Spirit intercedes for God's people in accordance with the will of God.*

**Chapter 6. Wait a week and we will get back with you.**

Since the mass in my abdomen was large and growing quickly, it was removed without knowing exactly what it was. We just knew it had to get out of there. After the surgery and immense pain, I was sent home to wait for results. This week of waiting was the first time I channeled Granny as I waited to hear my pathology reports. I am not sure what the typical wait time is on pathology. Each person you talk to will have a different story of when they were told and how they were told. Thank goodness in this world of technology I have not heard that any one has received a text with their diagnosis.

It's a funny thing. Doctors are very black and white and "just the facts" type of people. They use the word *cancer* as if it is as normal as *ice cream* or *vacation*. In all actuality, it is not at all normal and it needs to come with a warning label. *"WARNING: You are about to hear something that is going to turn your life upside down and change you dramatically physically, financially, spiritually, and mentally and you will never be the same again."* I am just saying that if we need to be warned that "coffee cups are hot," then a heads up on the "c" word would be nice.

On July 25, 2006, I called my gynecological oncologist, (aka Satan's Spawn's) office. I was told she was out of the office, but the nurse could confirm my pathology results were in fact lying on the doctor's desk. Unfortunately, I was also told a nurse was not able to tell me the results. Then, I was informed that this nurse had updated the surgeon of the results since she was out of the office. Satan's Spawn would be calling me to tell me the results herself. None of this information was particularly helpful, by the way. So, I tried another route. (Talk to me, Granny.)

I started feeling a tad feisty, and ready to go toe to toe with whoever got in my way. *Eureka!* I would call my OB/GYN and have her find out what was happening.

*Brilliant!*

I figured the oncology nurse would definitely talk with my doctor; that had to work. Unfortunately, I was told by my OB/GYN, "No, I am sorry, but they weren't able to tell me either." So, I just sat there staring into space, considering that a nurse and Satan's Spawn know my future, but I don't. They will go home with this information and make poisoned apples and sharpen their tridents, and I will just sit here. *How is this okay?* Honest to goodness, I can remember this in a weird out-of-body-experience kind of way. I can see myself sitting on the top of my deck stairs on a cool early evening thinking, *oh, shit...this can't be good.* I shared the information with Pete over supper and the optimistic fool said, "You don't have cancer. You will be fine. Please pass the stuffing." I seriously wanted to reach over and pat his knee and say "You poor, poor man. When did you become so delusional?" Instead, I said nothing and ate supper in silence, knowing in the depths of my being things had just gotten real...again.

When we wake up on any given day, we never have a clue of what is really going to happen. However, because most days are filled with mundane tasks, we never really stop and think *oh no, what will today bring?* Baz Luhrmann sums it up in his song, "Everybody's Free to Wear Sunscreen." He sings, *"The real troubles in your life are apt to be things that never crossed our worried mind; the kind that blindside you at 4pm on some idle Tuesday."*

Cue the Dragnet music because here comes the continuation of how life can throw you a curve ball.

The story you are about to read is true. The facts are different from the song because, well, this isn't a song. It's what really happened. You are going to be blindsided when you don't expect it. That is exactly what happened. Most of the time we are wrapped up worrying about the little things of life, when really the things that blow us out of the water are the things that never even crossed our minds as possible worries. Some people would say I am a worrier, and I would tell you I have lost some hours worrying. But never, never had I ever thought I would have cancer while I was pregnant.

*Matthew 24:36*
*"As for that day and hour, nobody knows it, neither the angels of heaven, nor the Son, no one but the Father alone."*

The end of the world, the end of our own lives, or the diagnosis of cancer…we don't know the hour when we are going to be blindsided. In later chapters, we will discuss a list of things we can all do today that will help us prepare for some of those earth shattering moments. As for me, the day was July 26, 2006, shortly after nine o'clock in the morning. It was a Wednesday (Buz was off by one day). The phone rings. It is *her.* She jumps right in with it. "You have cancer. It is stage 1a nueroblastoma teratoma." Pete is sitting across our living room on the other couch. His eyes are begging me for a sign of some kind. Thumbs up or down. Verbal recognition…anything. His face is pleading the words, "Throw me a bone, lady."

I had nothing for him. I was trying to ignore him and focus on these words that just kept rolling out of the receiver and tackling me, but again I said nothing. I did nothing. I sat and nothing was really making it through to a deeper understanding. There were just words, no, more like noises at this point. They weren't even words anymore. The conversation was one-sided and short. The call ended, and I hung up the phone, stunned. Pete who is always great at asking questions started firing away with, "What did she say?", "What does that mean?", and "What do we do next?" I stumbled through the answers that had no meaning to me; I was basically parroting the buffet of information that was dropped on my lap. Cancer. Stage 1a. Doctors didn't have a lot of answers. The tumor would be sent off for additional testing. More doctors would be gathering to discuss strategies. Pete hugged me and we were both introduced to the numb feeling of being utterly lost. There was silence, and nothing really to say. We really didn't have a direction. We were not given any kind of instruction or even resources to guide our next moves.

Doctors, my I please give you some more advice? Ask the patient if they have someone with them. If Pete wouldn't have been there to help, I really don't know what I would have done. I was in no shape to drive to get support if he had already left for work. Also, please ask to be on a conference call if possible so that more than one person hears the diagnosis. Ease into the conversation. After you drop the bomb shell please be ready with the next step. As a patient, I couldn't even form questions when I was told of my diagnosis. I would have appreciated just a quiet moment in the conversation to let it sink in. Then a comment like, "I'm sure you have lots of questions. Mrs. Peterson, I advise you to reach out to your family first and let them know that our next steps will be to ...Do you have any questions for me at this time? Remember, you can always reach my nurse at this number. I also want you to know Mrs. Peterson that we have a patient navigator/social worker on staff that can help you with finding support groups, professional services, and even beauty care like wigs and new hygiene routines. Do you have a pastor you could reach out to for support?" Having this human outreach would have made a world of difference. Fellow patients, keep this in mind as well when you start to make your phone calls, or however you tell your family and friends. Please don't drop the bombshell and leave them stranded. I realized that too late.

Unfortunately, Pete and I didn't have any direction and we got to a point in our bewilderment where there wasn't anything more to say or do. We did what we knew how to do. He headed to work and I made...*a list*, what else? Day one with cancer: make phone calls.

Remember, I am the youngest of five children. I moved through the phone calls methodically. I rationalized somehow who to call first. Ah, mom and dad, of course. My dad, who is notorious for not ever answering the phone, because then he will have to talk to people, actually picked up the receiver that day. I now had to tell the most unemotional person in my life I had cancer. That's not fair; let me take that back. Up to that point in my life he had shown a couple of emotions, but meeting my dad was like coming face-to-face with a morphed version of Archie Bunker and J.R. Ewing.

I didn't have time to think or plan; he wasn't supposed to answer the phone. So, I stalled for time and I said, "Is mom there? I have something I need to tell you both." He answered with the deep voice and curtness I actually find somewhat amusing. "Nope, she's in town. Can I know?" With shaking words, I threw it out into the universe for the second time in less than an hour. I hadn't put thought into it before dialing the numbers. I had just reeled back and threw it out there. This conversation was not long. I gave him a very quick rendition of the news from the morning. There wasn't much more to say and even on a good day the man has never been accused of having the gift to gab. He said, "Mom will call you later." I said, "Oh, okay. Sounds good." And we moved on. The good thing for me was that I got to move on to the next thing on my list.

Unfortunately for Dad, he was left by himself to ponder what all this meant. I can't imagine hearing your child has cancer and then being left alone to mull it over.

Later when mom called it was a down-to-business-fact-finding mission complete with planning and organizing. She volunteered to tell my oldest brother who was working on a welding crew in a nearby town. *Great*, I thought. That makes my list shorter and I understand the importance of her having something to do to keep her busy. That in itself is a wonderful lesson I learned. People will want to do things for you and your first reaction is, "No, I got this." Let them give this blessing to you. They want to help and need to be doing something to remain sane. It is a win-win situation. I have been on both sides of this scenario and if you can make a list of things you can release to someone else, you are truly doing everyone a huge favor.

When I got off the phone with my mom I went back to look at my list. I had things to do. Honestly, I do not recall the order of the other phone calls. I just remember parts of the conversations. To find my other brother who was currently moving around the country with the Air Force, I needed to call the Red Cross. *Well, that was a first. How many people say they have called the Red Cross?* (I saw the uniqueness of this opportunity even in the midst of chaos; it was yet another sign of my sick sense of humor.) I slowly dialed the number. I told a complete stranger I need to get a message to the Minot Air Force Base in Minot, North Dakota.

The receptionist asked ever so sweetly, "What's the message?"

I blurted out, "His sister has cancer." The words peppered the air like buck shot and slowly tore into my fragile ego.

"Oh, I'm sorry."

"Um yeah, thanks," was all I could muster. There was no elegance to my response, no composure.

The conversations were not getting easier, longer, or any classier. The words are there, and they are ugly. There was no editor or screenplay writer helping me along. It is just real life. The phrase, *"You can put lipstick on a pig, but it's still a pig,"* applies perfectly to this situation. Even if I would have glamorized it the facts were the same: gut wrenching. This may be why doctors just slap you with the words. They know it won't matter how the words are delivered; it will always feel like you have been hit by a truck.

I told one sister and she started making a list of things we could start taking care of before the baby arrived. *We. Must. Plan.* I nod. I agree. The conversation passed, and things were handled. Now my list was smaller. It was at about this point things were starting to spiral. I felt overwhelmed. I was moving, and things were happening, but there was a fog. Saying things out loud was starting to have a miserable effect on me. Something was changing.

In a different conversation, I heard myself ask another sibling, *"It sounds like you are in the car; can you pull over?"* There was a brief explanation and then I said, *"What can you do? I have no idea."* I had no answers. My list was done for the day and I didn't know what to do next. I couldn't tell her what to do because I had no idea what I was going to do. I could not even formulate a list for her by that time of day. I was stunned into silence and I just sat for a while. I had no voice. I was losing control of my well-organized life. Without a list, I was lost. It is at times like this that humans resort more often than not to food. This situation was no different. Before we ended the conversation, we made plans to go get ice cream.

It's odd what you remember and what slips into the blurry background of our life picture. I can still tell you where we went that night. I can tell you what booth we sat in, and I can tell you I ate chicken strips and a cherry dipped Dilly Bar and my sister had a mint chocolate Dilly Bar. There is something reassuring about sitting with people who don't have the answers either; to just sit and not talk about the elephant in the room. To talk about nonsense and not have a reality check until it is dark, the ice cream shop is closing, and goodbyes reluctantly need to be said. The hugs are strong and don't end. They say everything in the silence.

Thankfully I started a journal that night. Part of the first entry follows.

> *My mind reels with what this will all mean for me and secondly how will I, at the age of 28, do this? Raise a new baby, be a wife and survive cancer. This seems impossible. The outreach today from friends and family was amazing. They all said the same thing. "We'll do anything" and "You are strong enough to do this." Really? I who haven't been able to stick to anything in my whole life can now somehow take on THIS?! I'm scared and every time I say the words 'I have cancer' I think I am playing a role. I don't have cancer, but my character does. I've said all I want is a list to go by. Day one: call family and cry - done. Now what's day two? It's amazing how people react to things like this. My sister's tears. Mom's planning and Dad's fear. Then there is my rock Pete – well he's perfect and the buffet of emotions he showed was exactly the way true love is shown. I pray for the strength to live and move through tomorrow, Day 2. We meet with more doctors to figure out what comes next.*

No one ever gave me a list for day two or any day after that. It just became a ride down an unknown river. You just kind of go with the flow not really knowing if you are going in the right direction or not, nor do you know what lies ahead. It didn't take long before life got really exciting and the daily calendar was full of doctor appointments, planning, delivery, treatments and pure chaos. I remember one day when I was taking out the trash, I longed for things to be normal. I wanted the normal stresses and routine. I know that seems odd, but it's true. The day-to-day craziness we all live is what I craved. I remember saying, *"Well, I thought I was busy before."* There is no comparison to the busy feeling of a cancer patient/new mom/fighter for life. I know I am not alone in this. Recently, I heard a speaker share this Mary Jean Irion poem.

> *"Normal day, let me be aware of the treasure you are. Let me learn from you, love you, bless you before you depart. Let me not pass you by in quest of some rare and perfect tomorrow. Let me hold you while I may, for it may not always be so. One day I shall dig my nails into the earth, or bury my face in the pillow, or stretch myself taut, or raise my hands to the sky and want, more than all the world, your return."*

## Chapter 7: Day 2: Now What?

As far as I know, there is no word that adequately describes a human obsession to make lists. By making lists we allow a reprieve for our brains. On any normal day, our minds are tasked to remember a multitude of things. This seems to quadruple when we are thrown into the cancer world. New words like four syllable prescriptions, million-dollar procedure names, and diagnoses pelt us from every direction. It is hard to keep up. Making a focused and attainable list is a great way to get things done, and lists help remove the clutter in our heads, so we can concentrate on just one task. By simply having a breakdown of smaller tasks, the large job seems less daunting. The satisfaction of getting something off your list is pure joy if you ask me.

*People who want to appear clever rely on memory.*
*People who want to get things done rely on lists.*
*~Peter McWilliams*

On the second day of cancer, my to-do list was complete. I had no idea what to do or how to move forward. I kept thinking there had to be something I was supposed to be doing. With the hustle and bustle of everything going on, I couldn't see the forest for the trees, as they say. Even if I would have had the following list, I doubt I would have been able to make heads or tails of what was being said.

This is why it is important to have help in your inner circle and be able to trust friends and loved ones to be there for you. Every one of us has gifts to share. I challenge you to figure out which person you are going to be able to count on to help you with insurance companies and the paperwork. Have them sit with you and hear every question you are asking so there are two people hearing the answers.

It's time to get busy

1. Check with your health insurance carrier to confirm what the maximum out of pocket deductible is for the current year in your health plan. Then make sure to re-evaluate if you need to switch to a lower deductible plan next year knowing you are going to have a lot of claims. This will help with budgeting.
2. Make sure there aren't any pre-approval requirements for procedures or treatments that may not be covered by the insurance.
3. Update any wills or trusts to make sure all beneficiaries are properly listed and coordinate with your wishes as the patient. This is not being pessimistic; it's being smart and organized.
4. If you are not already doing so, sit down and make a budget, as this will help with the increased expenses that undoubtedly will occur.
5. Review all insurance policies to make sure beneficiaries are correct.
6. Review all disability insurance policies as most companies have    short term and long-term disability insurance that could come in handy if you need to be out of work.
7. Review any personal disability insurance policies to see if there are certain provisions for cancer and being out of work that would trigger a benefit event.

This is heavy and no fun, but it needs to be done, it gets you started on your way of taking charge. Do all of this while you are feeling strong because you won't want to do it once treatment starts.

Also, while you are feeling good and less ornery, I suggest making a list of the weekly and monthly chores you are willing to give up. People will be asking you what they can do for you, and you better have an answer other than "nothing." I suggest having them make a few calls for you and this will help life feel more organized.

1. Will your local grocery store allow you to shop online and have a neighbor pick it up for you?
2. Does your local dry cleaner make house calls?
3. Have a close friend call your veterinarian and groomer and ask what arrangements can be made for the upcoming appointments for Mittens and Daisy.
4. Maybe family members can call your church. Some churches require high school students to have volunteer hours. Can the students come and scoop snow, hang Christmas lights, rake leaves, plant flowers, paint, or mow?
5. While they have the church on the phone ask if you can be added to a prayer list.
6. Contact your local bank to see if they have a service to help send out monthly payments for you or sign up for automatic payments for your utilities.
7. Plan ahead and do some of the birthday and holiday shopping online or at least make a list of what you are going to need. Someone else can do the shopping and wrapping.

Check out the app todolist. Sick or healthy this is a great way to organize life. You can prepare for Christmas or a birthday party or make sure you have all your phone calls made and emails sent for the week. Take a deep breath and close your eyes. You do a lot and life feels like it is folding in on you now. You have a whole new list of things to tackle. Delegating is not easy for everyone. Know that people are willing to help and capable of handling things for you. Please try to slowly take things off your to do list and allow them to help and feel needed. Just remember that there will be somethings that no one will be able to take off your plate. For those things you will need to let go and let God.

*Let Go and Let God*
*By Lauretta P. Burns*

*As children bring their broken toys, with tears for us to mend. I brought my broken dreams to God, because He was my friend. But then, instead of leaving Him in peace to work alone. I hung around and tried to help, with ways that were my own. At last, I snatched them back and cried, "How can you be so slow?" "My child," He said, "What could I do? You never did let it go?"*

## Chapter 8:  July 26 in History

**1775** - United States Post Office (U.S.P.O.) was created in
Philadelphia under Benjamin Franklin.

**1805** - Naples/Calabria was struck by an earthquake; about
26,000 died.

**1848** - First Woman's Rights Convention (Seneca Falls, NY).

**1878** -  In California, the poet and American West outlaw
calling himself "Black Bart" made his last clean getaway
when he stole a safe box from a Wells Fargo stagecoach.
The empty box was found later with a taunting poem
inside.

**1897** - Thirty-seven-point-five-centimeter rainfall at Jewell,
Maryland for a state record.

**1903** - Horatio Nelson Jackson and Sewall K. Crocker
completed first automobile trip across the United States
(San Francisco to New York).

**1908** -  United States Attorney General Charles Joseph
Bonaparte issued an order to immediately staff the
Office of the Chief Examiner (later renamed the Federal
Bureau of Investigation).

**1918** - Race riot in Philadelphia (three whites and one black
killed).

**1928** - Yanks score 11 runs in 12th beating Tigers 12-1.

**1938** - First radio broadcast of "Young Widder Brown" on
NBC.

**1939** - Yankee catcher Bill Dickey hit three consecutive home runs.

**1943** - One hundred twenty degrees farenheit (49°C) in Tishmoningo, Oklahoma for a state record.

**1944** - Japanese suicide attack on U.S. lines in Guam.

**1946** - President Harry Truman ordered the desegregation of all U.S. forces.

**1955** - Ted Allen threw record 72 consecutive horseshoe ringers.

**1956**- Egypt seized the Suez Canal.

**1957**- Mickey Mantle hit career Home Run #200.

**1964** - U.S. union leader James Hoffa was sentenced for fraud.

**1967** - Twins beat Yankees 3-2 in 18 innings.

**1969**- Sharon Sites Adams, 39, became the first lady to solo sail the Pacific.

**1977** - USSR performed underground nuclear test.

**1979** - Estimated 109 centimeters (43") of rain fell in Alvin, TX for a national record.

**1983** - Jarmila Kratochvilova of Czech set the 800m woman's record (1:53.28).

**1990** - General Hospital recorded its 7,000th episode.

**1993** - Mars Observer took the first photo of Mars, from 5 billion kilometers.

**2005** - Space Shuttle program: STS-114 Mission - Launch of Discovery, NASA's first scheduled flight mission after the Columbia Disaster in 2003.

**2006** – Stacey Peterson diagnosed with stage 1a teratoma neuroblastoma.

**Teratoma:** "A type of germ cell tumor that may contain several different types of tissue and sometimes mature elements such as hair, muscle, and bone. Teratomas occur most often in the ovary, testis, and in the sacrococcygeal region (near the tailbone) in children. A teratoma may be benign or malignant" (Medcinenet.com).

**Neuroblastoma:** "Found in developing nerve cells of the medulla, this type of adrenal cancer usually affects infants or children under 10. Because of the nature of these types of cells, it can be easy to determine where they originated if detected early. However, in rare cases, since they can spread quickly, the origin can be hard to determine. According to the American Cancer Society, about one in three neuroblastomas begin in the adrenal glands."

Neuroblastoma accounts for approximately eight to ten percent of all tumors in children aged 15 years, and the incidence of neuroblastomas is one in 7000 in the United States. Primary ovarian neuroblastomas are extremely rare and have poor prognoses (ScienceDirect.com).

At this point you may want to take a break and pour yourself a strong and tall drink. I know I have that feeling when I read the science behind that date. After reading the explanation it doesn't make sense for this tumor to be in a 28-year-old pregnant lady, but it was. It was time to make a plan!

## Chapter 9: Angry Indeed.

*"You are making me angry! Very, very angry!"*
*~Warner Brothers Marvin the Martian*

Earlier in this book, I told you of the first surgery to remove the tumor and my left ovary. You may remember it was followed by the less than smooth post-op experience or "pain from hell." There was a ten-inch incision etched on my ever-growing belly. Pregnancy was not turning out the way the books, television, and now-a-days social media make it out to be. I would not be having one of those pictures where I show my ever-growing bare belly and my hands and Pete's hands make a heart. Looking at the scar I saw a monster, and the image of Frankenstein's Baby is not what I imagined in our baby book. Hormones, a dream being shattered, and my lack of patience all met up in a cacophonous eruption.

Back to the week of diagnosis: Finally, I had a face-to-face conversation with my least favorite oncologist. However, it was not her idea. It was one more time when I sat back and laughed at Pete's reaction to his emotional pregnant wife. He had finished work early and innocently came home to find that the lack of answers had taken its toll on me. I was angry, and I had snapped. I met him at the door and I told him to get back in the car because *"we were going down to that woman's office and we were getting some answers!"* He wisely turned around and we left immediately.

When we walked into the office it was completely empty besides the receptionist who was startled to see us barge in at 4:50 PM. We stated our business and she told us to sit down. Eventually we were brought back to the doctor's office, and we were given very dark details.

During this meeting, we found out that there had been two

women with similar diagnoses to mine. However, neither of these women were pregnant at the time of their diagnosis; consequently, my oncologist still didn't have a relevant treatment plan for me. The news from the two women was bleak. One had passed away and the other women had "lost contact" with the doctors. Our prognosis, though it was never really spelled out for us, was daunting. It was decided that both the baby and I would have specialists. The neonatal doctors were still trying to figure out what the best scenario was for our baby. Research showed that by me receiving steroid shots to boost the growth of the baby's lungs and continuing with the pregnancy to 32 weeks would leave us with a viable plan. This meant that my own treatment plan would be put on hold, which was not a typical scenario for most cancer patients.

As I have stated, the mass and ovary were removed as a first step for treatment. This is typically referred to as debulking. There was a pelvic wash, but lymph nodes would not be tested until the time of delivery to see if the cancer was spreading. The other snafu was that chemotherapy is typically done sooner rather than later on cancer patients. The pregnancy was really throwing a curve ball in those plans.

The tumor they removed was sent to Duke, MD Anderson, Mayo Clinic; and UCLA. The odd thing about my particular diagnosis, besides that it was found when I was 26 weeks pregnant, was that a neuroblastoma is typically found in children under the age of eighteen, not in a 28-year-old. Therefore, there was confusion about what to do with me, which was unsettling to say the least. Later in the process, I even had a child oncologist tell me I could do my treatment at the Children's Hospital since they were more familiar with my kind of tumor.

Satan's Spawn, who obviously did not like having people come in without an appointment and make her late for drinks at the country club, could see this unnerving information had me shaken. She used this opportunity to pounce. She looked at me with a dry smirk and dead eyes and said, "You seem pretty feisty; I bet you can handle it."

In my head I was saying, *What the F\*!# did you just say?* Let me get this right. Because I was tired of sitting at home, waiting for callbacks and not having answers about the direction my life was going, and I felt the only option to get more results on my condition was to come to your office for answers, that makes me feisty? *Really? Crazy me, I see it differently.* I see a woman who isn't doing her job and finds enjoyment in messing with the meek.

Granny?

Marvin the Martian?

I didn't know for sure. I just knew I was angry, but again I said nothing. I had never been spoken to like this. I had never met a mean girl of this caliber. It is a fact that volleying this kind of passive-aggressive malarkey has never been my strong suit. I do my best to avoid confrontations. I am not wired to deal with these types of personalities. I am always shocked by people who are blatantly rude. We left shortly after she gave us some verbal pats on the head. Pete and I staggered out of the office, and we went home to wait. I started to recount the afternoon's events. I had been stunned into silence. I struggled to wrap my brain around what just happened. The news of the medical information was enough to make me sick. Doctors had no idea what to do with me. That, combined with the lack of regard by my doctor had my head spinning. I was scheduled to see her soon to get the staples removed from my first surgery, and the time was dwindling on how many more times I could be attacked by this woman.

The incision healed rather quickly and when we needed to go in to remove the over-ninety staples on my ever-growing stomach, she figuratively punched me again. Now, I say over ninety staples because at 90 I stopped counting how many staples were clinking into the metal pan. For some reason, I had thought this not-so-great moment would go faster if I distracted myself with something. Unfortunately, the first thing I came up with was *let's count the snipping noises, tugging, and clinking of staples into the collection tin.* I couldn't go on after ninety. I then turned to what many patients resort to: I started counting the holes in the ceiling tiles.

Decorating tip number one for all doctors' offices: the recessed ceiling tiles every hospital has are boring to say the least. They all look the same and the scattered patterns of holes are too tempting not to count. I am strongly suggesting if for any reason your patient is going to be looking at the ceiling for a prolonged amount of time, do some simple decorating or interesting color schemes. It will do wonders for your patient's mental state.

Finally, we were done with the removal of staples and I was assured I had healed well. At that time Satan's Spawn had yet another trick up her sleeve. She ever so innocently asked a humane question about my plans for the birth of my child. I let my guard down and relished in the idea of my baby coming into this world. Finally, I was distracted by happy thoughts! I told her I was not yet sure of my birthing plan. With a smug look on her face and a flawless switch of emotions she suggested to me, "Well, you don't handle pain very well, so you should have an epidural." And she walked out. A shocked *oh no you didn't look* spread across my face. I turned to Pete and asked if I just heard her correctly. Again the "Ah, Laud" look invaded his features because he knows me too well. The mild-mannered woman he had been married to for five years was slipping away. Granny was surfacing. He knew he should be afraid. Very afraid.

*Tuck and roll, man, tuck and roll!*

He knew the next few hours would consist of me having bursts of uncontrollable comebacks and rants indicative to a sailor. *Sorry mom.* When she left that room that day, she had just set him up for the unbridled fury that lives within my five-foot five-inch frame. She was a crafty rascal; that's for sure.

Looking back through my medical records I am able to read some of the dialogue these doctors from all over the country were having about my removed tumor.

> *"The histologic sections demonstrate extensive areas of immature differentiation which I would characterize as neuroblastoma. Even the highly cellular areas demonstrate focal neuroendocrine staining. This pattern is uncommon in my experience. I found an article in the American Journal of Surgical Pathology describing primary neuroectodermal tumors of ovary. Many of these are associated with teratomas. Only two in this series were classified as neuroblastoma. One was lost to follow-up and the other died seven months later. There are a few scattered case reports for this patient."* ~MD in Pathology in South Dakota. Recommend sending it to Mayo.

> *"Since her ovarian tumor is very rare, it is going to be treated as a neuroblastoma."* ~ OB/GYN

There was not a lot of information and there were many unknowns about my tumor. Doctors from all over the country were sitting around conference tables talking about this and scratching their heads.

I tell you all of that to make my point.

Medically speaking, you will need to find your voice. It will come in handy when options for treatments are brought to you. It is important you trust your doctor; I can't say that enough. I am not necessarily talking about having the best surgeon on paper. I found it equally important to find someone who showed genuine human characteristics. Please understand that trusting your doctor doesn't mean you go through the motions blindly taking medications and agreeing to surgeries. On the contrary, I want you to feel comfortable enough to ask questions and trust the answers. Make sure you understand their recommendations for you. Remember every patient is not created equally, and knowing why a regimen is chosen for you is important. Ask what other options there are and understand the procedures. Empowerment is a wonderful tool for you to have to beat this disease.

I want to remind you to bring someone with you on your doctor visits. Comprehending medical information is overwhelming even when we are getting the regimen for taking the simplest medications. Do I take it with food or not? Is it refrigerated? When do I take it…etc.? Now multiply that by, I don't know, a thousand, and now you are close to understanding what it is like when you are hearing about your cancer protocol. Make sure one of you brings a tablet and pen because, (here it comes), *you will need to start making a list* and you will want to start writing down questions, concerns, and general ideas from the doctor. *Ta-da!*

As we move into more of my diagnosis, you can see that my first piece of advice, "Get Ornery," comes in handy. There is one thing about being ornery you need to understand. There will be someone in your life, you know who they are, who will start telling you how to do things. They mean well, I know, but honestly you are going to want to punch them in the throat. At this point in your diagnosis, you have the right not to shower today or to eat leftovers for breakfast because it is what finally tastes good.

I truly believe; however, you're getting through this moment is perfectly okay. There will be a moment…wait for it…maybe it's now, that you do feel like pulling yourself up by the bootstraps and kicking butt. The fact is some days you won't. It's okay. Harness your orneriness, use the cancer card and your voice, and tell that person, *No!* because they just aren't getting it. They don't know what you are feeling. Get ornery and say what you gotta say to get that privacy, get the snack you want, or to get the peace you desire. Then, get ornery with yourself and move past any self-pity. There will be days to eat leftovers in sweats and there will be days you shower and go for a walk. Getting ornery isn't just a weapon to be used on others, sometimes it's what we need to prescribe for ourselves.

I learned during the cancer process the old cliché is right: life is short. I have never been good with politics and giving the 'no-answer answers.' Because truthfully *ain't nobody got time for that.* (Thank you, YouTube, for that urban gem.) I'm a straight shooter. Take it or leave it. That is me. My face always gives me away. Don't get me wrong; I'm not barbaric. I don't even think I'm mean. I just want to *keep it real* as often as I can. (A little something again for those young readers, wink-wink.) Anything else is way too draining for me. In my opinion, while you are going through diagnoses, treatment or life in general, there isn't time for games. Not *those* games anyway. I am always up for a good game of Scattegories© though. Know that being true to yourself and up front with the people around you, will make this cancer trip easier.

Now, some of you may say the reason I don't like these games or politics is because I don't play those mind games well. Fact: you nailed it on the head. I don't, but it's no secret; I don't want to be good at those games. If I say, "let's get together soon," then I mean let's get together. If I say, "I will see you at five o'clock," then I mean five fifteen at the latest. If I say, "I don't feel like walking around this floor one more time in my dignity-free hospital gown," then I mean "Now is not a good time." I have put my foot down.

## Is that you, Granny?

One "aha" moment I experienced came when I was talking with a photographer friend. She asked how I was doing and my answer blew her away. As I mentioned, I started seeing life differently than most 28-year-olds, or at least differently than I had ever before. I was realizing just how precious life was and how short of a time we have here on Earth. I told her I was feeling fine, but I was starting to feel consumed with anxiety when I thought about only having sixty years or so left with my baby. *Only sixty years.* Up to that point in my life, I was like most people who think living to my late eighties would be plenty of time to do everything I needed. I had suddenly realized, seeing my child for sixty years just wasn't enough. Life is short and when I think how long I will be dead versus how many years I am alive, it seemed heart breaking. I have a short time to make my impact, to laugh, to get my point across, and to one day finally finish a Sudoku puzzle. So, if I am ornerier than you think I should be, go stick it in your ear. I earned this orneriness.

## Chapter 10: Having Faith

For just a moment I'd like to suggest we put a figurative bookmark in the cancer part of my story and focus on the fun part of this story: the pregnancy.

The room had been painted and a whimsical farm theme was chosen. The crib was assembled, reassembled and then assembled again due to bad planning and skinny doorways. Registries were organized and there were moments of down time or normal time to think about baby names.

I think it's normal for expecting parents to sit and talk about what features they hope their new bundle of joy will inherit. We had discussed genetics up one wall and down the other even using a mathematical equation to figure out the adult height of our baby. Fingers crossed, we are hoping for at least 5'6". Sorry Faith, that's my fault.

Names had not been a main focus yet. We played the Rachel and Ross game from *Friends* of vetoing names. This is classic because it is during this monumental time in every pregnancy when people are reminded of the creepy kid in fifth grade who would wipe his armpits with his hand after gym class and then lick said hand.

"We can't name him ……"

"Well, we aren't naming her …."

Never once in our volleying of names did we ever come up with Faith. Not once. We had decided on a girl and boy name and we were content. We figured more names would come, but we were thrilled we could agree on at least one for each gender. Then weirdly out of the blue one day after all the nonsense started the name Faith was suddenly on the table. It's odd because it was such a random thought, *but boy did it fit*. That's how the Holy Spirit works, though. When we aren't really looking, an idea is placed deep in our hearts. That idea is so much better than anything we could come up with on our own.

I remember sitting down with my sister and niece having one of those girly talks that have always been very odd to me, when this name-choosing topic arose. I threw out our name suggestions to see if they would be accepted. Then out of curiosity I asked this question: *"What you think about the name Faith?"* Then with a personality that explains why we get along so well, my sister responded, "Considering everything that is going on, it sounds better than naming her *HOLY CRAP*." Yes, my pregnancy could have been summed up with those two words as well.

"This is our child, Holy Crap."

"Oh my, what a unique name."

"Why thank you. We thought of it when I was diagnosed with cancer during pregnancy."

However, I think we can all agree we chose the name that fits better in social gatherings, yet helps us sum up our mental state as we prepared to bring Faith Ann into the world. I never get tired of the look on people's faces when they hear our story, and they put two and two together and figure out why we named our baby Faith. I often joke about this wonderfully inspired name and how it made it impossible for us to have more children. Faith has a wonderful story, one she is very proud to tell. Can you imagine the sibling rivalry when her humble brother Bob was born?

Faith: "I was with mom through the most difficult time of her life."

Bob: "Well, um my name can also be a verb!"

Faith: "My name means completely trusting."

Bob: "My name means ……um."

Faith: "My name is defined in the book of Hebrews as the substance of things hoped for, the evidence of things not seen."

Bob: "Shut up!"

**Chapter 11: Let's keep it simple.**

When I started compiling ideas for this book nearly eight years after my cancer diagnosis, I started with a small notepad I kept in the console of my car. I would jot down different things that made me happy. I had done something similar when I was a teacher. I called it my smile file.

Now, I was making a list of things that brought me pure joy just by reading them in a list. I was not experiencing them personally, but just reading the words. My list was born as I joined the other anxious and caffeine-driven mothers outside of our children's hip-hop dance class. As class would near it's end, I began to think and to dread what the next forty minutes was going to look like. Parents were all doing the same thing. We sat there looking at our cell phones every minute and a half waiting for class to be done. At that ever-anticipated moment when the door creaked open and the first child emerged, we nabbed them and performed NFL running back-type moves to successfully maneuver through the crowds back out into civilization. We became drill sergeants mixed equally with high school coaches urging our children by muttering "MOVE! MOVE! MOVE!" through clinched teeth and by cursing at the traffic around us, as we practiced our math facts, spelling words and squeezed in some time to listen to what happened at recess. This was all done as we weaved through traffic to make it, just in time, to the next event.

It was now eight years from diagnosis and life had gotten pretty "normal" again. The Holy Spirit had urged me several times to start writing my thoughts down, but I was stubborn. I resisted and had a hundred different reasons why these urges were anything but the Holy Spirit. Through all the multi-tasking, hurdling and constant thrashing I battled with the urges to write and the doubts of what I would say. Eventually, during those almost daily sprints from one event to the next, I yearned to get to the computer and tell you how important it is to slow down and appreciate the small things in life: irony at its best. Yes, I find that pretty funny. I have a messed-up sense of humor - it's what gets me through most of my days, and you will need one too as you tackle the biggest opponent you have met thus far. So, here it goes in no particular order.

The simple things in life....
1. Television shows that (a) start with the deep and theatrical voice of the male announcer… "Previously on …" or (b) shows that tease with this week's program and then immediately goes into the music. Or lastly, (c) which is equally fulfilling, television shows where there is music and directly into the show. No waiting! Gotta love it!
2. Succinct homilies.
3. Clothes you slip on right out of the dryer. Mmmm warm!
4. Sun tea, (none of that sweet tea, either).
5. Oh, I forgot option (d): Television shows with catchy theme songs, and (e) Television programs that preview next week's show. These are also ranked high in my book. Get it… in my book?!
6. Animals that are dressed up - personally I want a duck with a bow tie or a goat with a hat.
7. Coupons.
8. 72 degrees.
9. Finding money in your pockets. It makes you ask the question, "Are these even my pants?"
10. When you try on spring clothes after a long winter and everything still fits. Am I right, ladies?
11. Naps.
12. Naps in the sun.
13. Crawling into bed and snuggling into cool sheets - especially when you lay your newly-bald head on a cool satin sheet for the first time!
14. An unexpected package in the mail.

15. Audio books - I don't care what you say; it is reading!
16. Short emails.
17. The sound of flip flops.
18. Rain storms.
19. Snow days, even the anticipation of a snow day.
20. Slippers.
21. Rugs with extra cushion so when you step down your foot almost disappears.
22. Heated towels after a shower.
23. Walks.
24. Eating outside at a restaurant!
25. An elderly person's hands.
26. Antique stores.
27. Small towns, then leaving a small town.
28. Voiding one's bladder.
29. Back roads.
30. Eating dirty carrots from a garden. It is <u>not</u> gross!
31. Alarm free mornings.
32. Baby shoes.
33. Baby toes.
34. Curls at the nape of my daughter's neck when it's humid.
35. Decorated trees.
36. <u>Dill</u> pickles.
37. Stain glass windows.
38. The color yellow.
39. Lilies.
40. Football season.
41. Traditions.
42. The smell of horses.
43. Baby goats, even better: baby goats wearing a hat.
44. GOOD hugs. You know the ones I'm talkin' 'bout.
45. Songs that help you spell words.
46. Finding change on the ground.
47. Getting two vending machine snacks when you only put money in for one.

48. A good dog.
49. When a child takes your hand.
50. An open parking spot when you are in a hurry.
51. The smell of suntan lotion.
52. Mello Yello - if you don't know, look it up.
53. Watching your child have their moment in the spotlight.
54. No lines.
55. Lists.

## Chapter 12:  Cue the music:  Introducing the Superhero

You have met the main character and the villain. Now, it is time for the superhero to come and save the day. Cue the music!

It was late August 2006. Our baby was born eight weeks early. I made the decision to finally switch oncologists and hospitals. This part of the journey started with us going into yet another waiting room and filling out another round of exhausting paperwork. We were surrounded by "old" women. The average age for an ovarian cancer patient is 63 according to the American Cancer Society website, and let's just say I didn't feel like I was in a room with my peers. I was having a moment of *I don't belong here.* Please understand up to this point, I hadn't been only the patient. I was able to focus on the baby's needs, and I could hang out with pregnant women in a fun waiting room that was brightly painted and welcoming. No one could tell anything else was going on and I fit in. Now, I was *the* patient. The focus was all on me and I suddenly realized I was not the typical patient for this disease. I was sitting in a pretty elegant waiting room with large windows, a fireplace, muted area rugs and interesting artwork. It lacked the joy of baby animals being pulled on a train across the wall though. My new waiting room buddies weren't as comfortable to sit with in comparison to those in the obstetrics office. No one was making eye contact and there was no small talk.

Then this boisterous tan man in a white lab coat came bounding through the waiting room complaining about how his voice recorder wasn't working properly. He had a Magnum PI mustache and large black framed glasses. He wasn't that much taller than me, but he seemed to carry so much power. He turned sheepishly to see all of us sitting in his worldly decorated waiting area and he came straight over to me. Still with his roaring voice and Palestinian accent he said, "You must be Stacey. Stacey, Stacey, Stacey. That's all I've heard about this week!" At that moment, I was sure I had made a grave mistake and thought for a second maybe Satan's Spawn wasn't so bad. Then Dr. Samir leaned in closely, so I was the only one who could hear him, and he said the single thing that allowed me to breathe and sink into the foreign feeling I used to know as comfort. He whispered, "I know what we are going to do." The rest of the room was gone to me. I have no idea what anyone else was doing or if there was any noise. I just remember his closeness, his confidence and the ease with which I surrendered to his care. Eight words. I finally felt control come back into my life with those eight simple words.

Life lesson # 65 for every villain in your life there will be a superhero.

While talking with Dr. Samir we got answers. He gave us hope saying, "When you decide you are done having children, we will do a hysterectomy." He was a surgeon who didn't want to cut unless it was needed, and that is rare and almost unheard of nowadays. At that point in my life I wasn't ready to make that choice. I had just given life to our first child. I was a month away from my 29th birthday. I was facing a scary diagnosis and was in no frame of mind to decide what shoes to wear, not to mention what organ to remove. He never pushed the point and for that I will never be able to share adequately my gratitude. He was patient and he knew I was in no place to be making life-changing decisions. The plan was to send me through chemotherapy as protocol, even though my lymph nodes were clear from any cancer.

Chemo was going to be harsh on my remaining ovary. Dr. Samir did something else to blow me away; he was always surprising me. He recommended I go back to the other hospital in town, the competition, to talk with a fertility doctor. He said the best fertility doctor for me was at the other hospital. Recommending me to him was the best thing for me in his opinion. He regularly said, "If you were my daughter…." No politics, he was striving for the best treatment. This was 180 degrees from the other advice I had gotten. My previous oncologist told me shortly after the birth of my child, "Be happy you have one healthy baby because chemotherapy will probably make you infertile." *Boom!* Those are the words she chose to use with a hormonal new mom and cancer patient. By having Dr. Samir's advice of talking with a fertility doctor, I was given the option to take shots during chemotherapy to buy myself time and try to remain in control. Options. Control. Hello, dear friends. Dr. Samir was starting to put my life back together. He was righting my ship.

After meeting with Dr. Samir that day and getting initial questions answered, I was scheduled for surgery and a port-a-cath was inserted by my right clavicle. A port is about an inch to inch and a half in diameter and it is installed beneath the skin as a way to administer intravenous drugs quickly. Blood samples can be drawn from the port as well and it is supposed to be less painful than receiving constant needle pricks. From September 11, 2006 until the middle of October, life was pretty normal for a cancer patient.

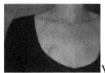 yahoo images of a port-a-cath

Even looking at this image today I have an unsettled feeling. I hated feeling that foreign body under my skin. I couldn't stand seeing it or the scar that accompanied it. Looking at it made me feel robotic or less human somehow. I was very self-conscious, and it took years for the scare to fade into my complexion. It's interesting to look back on the journal entry I wrote from

September 11, 2006.

*Surgery again, this time to get my port-a-cath. I was
more nervous about having another surgery than I
realistically should have been. I am just tired of doctors.
We watched all the memorials on T.V. for the September
eleventh 5th year anniversary to help me stay distracted.
(I guess it was a way to keep things in perspective.)
After surgery, my biggest complaint was a sore neck that
came from the position they put me in for the surgery.
After I awoke, the surgery wasn't as bad as I expected.
We were off to Dr. Samir's office. First a pelvic exam
and now, by this time I was tired of waiting and tired of
being poked and/or worrying so I grumbled, "Let's get
this done." The sooner we started, the sooner we could
finish. Walking into the treatment room I was met with
the same feeling I had entering every swim lesson I ever
went to, my college orientation and the first day of work
at any job.
Everyone looks at you and you feel like there is a
flashing light above your head, "Hey, I'm the new guy!"
I had been tired of waiting for it all to start, but in the
moment of actually walking into the chemotherapy room
I realized I was not truly ready for it.*

Picture the Wizard of Oz when the lion with his mane done in a
bow, tries to build enough courage to address the Wizard. He is
strongly reprimanded and takes off down the hallway and jumps
out the window. *That* is how it feels! "Tell me when it's over
(sob, sob). I want to go home!"

The treatment room had recliners in it that made a "c" shape in
front of a television. The idea was for patients to sit and be
pumped full of chemicals while they watch the *Price is Right,* as
if we were at home in our own living rooms. I hated it. I would
always bring a bag of things to distract myself. Brain numbing
magazines, my journal, cards so I could send thank yous, a
blanket and a light lunch. I never felt like eating, the television

never had what I wanted to watch, and I could never focus. So, I would usually bury my head under my blanket and take a nap. It was lonely. It was scary and all I wanted to do was step out of this role. *Oh, understudy? Stunt double? Where are you guys?* I was scheduled to do chemotherapy for nine weeks straight. I would do five days of chemo, relax over the weekend and then get a long session on the following Monday. I'd get the rest of the week off to regroup and then do a full week again. The Monday after the full week was always the hardest. The weekend just wasn't enough time to bounce back from the ugliness that is chemotherapy. The recipe or protocol for every cancer patient is different. I have found over the years people want to compare notes on what drugs they were given. They rattle it off as normal behavior and simple jargon. "I was cisplatin and paclitaxel," and then with a smug sniff and a slight rise of the chin, "What were you?"

It's the most awkward sorority password confirmation for an undercover gang ever. I am not sure why this exchange of recipes is so important, but it happens every time I meet a fellow survivor. It is awkward every time, too, because I have no clue of the answer. Dr. Samir had simplified it into an acronym and I never thought it was that important for me to remember.

[Grunt] "Drugs good."
[Hrumph, scratch, sniff] "Mean survival."

I was like a pickled drinker, "Hit me! Just give me the good stuff and get on with the show. Where, hic wh-where are the preddy fellas? Hic. Turn up the music? Bow chica whow whow."

I was just going through the motions and not paying attention to all the details. I really didn't think that was my job. The doctors and nurses needed to know not me. For me it was *load me up. I want to go home.* I wish Dr. Samir had shown me the secret handshake and the special knock to get in. Now, to get into the special meetings I have to resort to lifting my shirt and showing my scar because I can't remember the chemotherapy drug names.

For those of you who need to know the hard facts, I went in and dug up my personal recipe: Bleomycin/Etoposide/Cisplatin was my concoction. It really isn't something that roles off the tongue so maybe you can see why I have had a hard time putting it into long term memory. Like everyone else I was given steroids and anti-nausea medicine before the chemo drugs were administered. I handled the first course of chemotherapy well and started to get buckled up for the bumpy ride.

*Fasten your seat belts, please, and know that your floatation device will be worthless.*

As I read back through my journal for this time of my life, I have confirmation that things were fine. No major problems, just a little gastrointestinal discomfort. My 29th birthday passed, and I was more concerned about my white blood count than the numbers in my age. Chemotherapy is determined to kill all cells, and this includes your white cells, which help to defend your body against infections and disease. Having numbers too low would mean I could take a day off from chemo in hopes the time away would allow the white cells to regenerate on their own.

I was reassured this dance was normal and it wouldn't be a backwards step in my overall treatment. At the beginning of October, I was about a month into my treatment. I was staying regularly at a "2-2.3" or 2000-2300 white blood cells per milliliter of blood. This is low for the typical person, but it is very normal for a person who is going through chemotherapy to have these kinds of results. Low white blood cell counts can become a problem because patients are more susceptible to infections. Some cancer patients are extremely careful during this time and will limit visitors and trips to social arenas. Cancer patients are encouraged to have the flu vaccine to ensure they are well protected during their treatment.

To combat the dropping white blood cell numbers, scientists have found giving patients a shot of a bone marrow stimulant will increase their numbers while allowing them to feel every pulse that goes through their body. No lie, especially large bones like those in your leg. This process allows patients to be physically ready for chemotherapy again. During this dreaded time, I was not thankful to these scientists. They were making me better so I could go have more poison pumped into me. *Oh joy!*

Getting this shot was an education all in itself. The weirdest sensation for me was when all the large bones in my body would ache and I was able to feel my heartbeat in them. The other odd side effect was it hurt to chew food; with each bite the contact with food would cause pain in my jaw no matter how gingerly I bit down. The shots worked, though, and I was over 9000 white blood cells by Monday: ready for more chemo! *Yea... I guess.*

During this time, I was also getting ready to deal with the loss of my hair. As you may have figured out from the set-up of this book, I am a planner. I figured I would get ahead of this hair loss game. I had my dear friend and my hair stylist come over to the house and give me a new style. The idea was this would be a great way for me to get used to a shorter look. I had long hair my whole life, and this above-shoulder-do was a big step. I was also thinking it would be a way for me to let the public see this short look before I whipped out my wig that had a similar look. I just wanted to progress from my hair to the wig as calmly and fluently as possible. In my delusion no one was going to know I was a cancer patient. This was important to me. I didn't want people seeing me sick. I didn't want my secret out there for everyone. I didn't want to be looked at.

Exactly fourteen days from my first treatment I started to lose my hair. Beautiful fall days of me driving with the windows open would cause a matted mess on the headrest of my car. It was a race between my hair and the foliage outside. What would fall to the ground faster?

I would comb through my hair waiting for the moment when the brush would stop collecting hair. That didn't happen though. With every stroke more hair came out. Waking up to a pile of hair on my pillow or in the towel while I dried my hair was hard. I don't think Pete ever saw this. I tried very hard to clean it up before he would have a chance to see the mess. Nothing has ever measured up to when I would snuggle up with my baby, all wrapped in pink, and *that* moment being ruined when she reached for me and hair came out in her hand.

Up to that point in my life I had never considered myself to be vain. As women, though, our hair defines us. Losing my hair was an emotional blow I certainly was not expecting. Years later when Faith was three, her long beautiful curly sandy blond hair was long enough to donate to a foundation that would turn the donated hair into wigs for cancer patients. Even though we had started growing our hair out at the same time, I had chosen to embrace a shorter hairstyle for a while. When she was three it was easy to convince her that cutting her hair for others was a good thing. She was all for it until the nice lady couldn't reattach the ponytail. (Oh, the mind of a three-year-old.) *See image at the end of this chapter.

At the time, the easiest way to explain to her why people lost their hair was because the medicine that was saving their lives was making their hair fall out. I remember seeing the wheels turn in her young mind and the question slowly forming: would the occasional medicines she took for allergies or tooth pain cause her hair to fall out? I love watching a child's mind make sense of adult subjects. To this day Faith still explains chemotherapy as a medicine that helps cancer patients, but makes their hair fall out. I found a more scientific way of explaining this side effect on breastcancer.org.

Hair loss occurs because chemotherapy targets all rapidly dividing cells—healthy cells as well as cancer cells. Hair follicles, the structures in the skin filled with tiny blood vessels that make hair, are some of the fastest-growing cells in the body, so they are impacted first.

I will talk more about the hair in a bit. I really started to dread my trips for chemo. The doctor's office was on the third floor and there was only one time I actually took the elevator. I would do anything to slow myself down to delay my arriving to the office. I knew on a mature and reasonable level chemo was saving my life. I knew that hundreds of thousands of people do it. That didn't mean I had to like it. I never had the really bad gastrointestinal issues I feared would come. It wasn't even a pity party of *why me*? I was just sick and tired of being sick and tired. I didn't like going. I didn't like the environment and I didn't like the side effects. I just didn't want to go anymore. There was one day when Pete dropped me off at the automatic doors and pulled out into the circular drive only to see me sitting on the bench as he circled around. Confused, he continued turning the wheel into a full circle easing up to me on the bench. He rolled down the passenger window and asked, "Are you going to go in?"

I felt like a child, but I *really* didn't want to go. I mean we have seen the jokes about calling in sick for work. Well, this was my work and I was really getting tired of it and technically I was sick. My "co-workers" were complaining and it really brought me down. I was the new kid and couldn't really relate to anybody. Many times I would come in, sit down, wait to be hooked up to my machines and then cover my head and sleep. It was an ugly time, and I am not proud of how I dealt with it. I wish I could say I came into chemo with cookies and cracking jokes... pointing at the others with my thumb and forefinger, winking and saying, "We need to stop meeting this way!" You know, the combination of Patch Adams and a juggler that makes everyone's day, being able to pull quarters from behind the nurse's ear, but I just wasn't that patient. I came. I was treated. I went.

I wish I could even say I was so strong through chemo that I worked like many cancer patients do, but again I was not that patient. I was on maternity leave. I wish I could say I was up every four hours breastfeeding my baby, but I can't say that. I was having poison injected into my body and wasn't able to be the mom I had pictured either. I was tired, and was recuperating from surgeries and chemotherapy. I just couldn't do anything a new mom does. I want to say I was amazing and inspirational, and after a day of chemo I was able to cook supper and give my baby a bath and dote on her, changing her outfits every fifteen minutes just to play dress up. Instead I was tired and weak. I was not being a wife or a mother. I was miserable. Dr. Samir saw this and recommended I talk to someone.

I did do a little bit of counseling at this point. I would recommend to anyone dealing with any new situation to find a group for support. In my situation, I had a few *groups* I could have talked to. Being a new mom, I should have sought out some new moms to gain support for the baby blues. It's real, and hearing I wasn't alone may have helped. I really should have found a support group for the cancer. I saw flyers and could have visited the resource library at the hospital to find a young cancer group or even an ovarian cancer specific group. This would have helped me to understand some of my feelings and see that what I was feeling was completely normal. I would have been able to share my burdens and been inspired to be the patient I had created in my mind.

Instead of a support group I followed Dr. Samir's' recommendation and started talking with a psychologist. When I first sat down with the counselor and explained the last couple of months of my life, I internally smiled to see her shock. I was a combination not found in the text books. Should she help me through the guilt of not being able to be a mom? The post-partum depression? The denial, fear and tragedy of learning to cope with being a cancer patient? I was just one of those messes you aren't sure how to approach the clean-up.

The ultimate *where do we start?*

Therapy didn't last too long because by the end of October - just seven weeks into my chemotherapy - I was going to throw another curve ball at the medical world. My life was never boring.

\*\*\*

Faith after the haircut; a little teary eyed and apprehensive.

## Chapter 13:  Comfort Items

Over the last few years there have been different opportunities
when either a friend or I needed to purchase a thoughtful gift for
a newly diagnosed cancer patient. I started to make a list of
things that I remember getting and things I wished I had gotten.
One direction you may want to go is finding the correct cancer
color for the patient and getting a scarf, shirt, jewelry, or blanket
in that color. Every cancer, and I think at this point every cause,
has a ribbon color. Leukemia awareness is celebrated with
orange. Prostate cancer ribbons are a light blue. Throat cancer is
a beautiful combination ribbon of burgundy and white. More
than likely the patient will at some point be in a social situation
when they will want to support this new organization into which
they have been baptized.

During our difficult time, there were many people reaching out
and asking to help our family. Pete's work schedule and his
understanding coworkers made it easier for him to take me to
therapy sessions. We were asked regularly how people could
help us, and there were a few times we would allow others to
help. I say it like that because unintentionally we were bound
and determined we weren't going to rely on anyone. We could
do this. In my opinion, it is one of the biggest mistakes, but one
of the most common mistakes humans make when their world is
being turned upside down. I would like to strongly urge you to
fight this feeling to keep people out. By pushing them away you
are denying them the chance to bless you and feel needed. To be
on the outside with your hands tied and being pushed away is so
defeating. If you allow them to bring a meal, drive you to an
appointment or pick up your dry cleaning, you are creating the
best win-win situation.

May I also suggest, if you are on the receiving end of the
strong-arm tactic, keep trying. If the patient and their family
won't let you in, then figure it out on your own. Ask yourself

what demands *your* own attention on a daily or weekly basis? The cancer patient still has all those responsibilities and is dealing with the cancer issues, too. Here are a few categories that might come to mind and how you can help the family without feeling like you are constantly bothering them. Figure out how you are going to help and tell the patient or the family how you will be blessing them.

1. An extremely soft and warm blanket - great for chills during chemo and support during hard days.
2. A satin pillow case - it feels amazing on a bald head.
3. Imodium* (nurse recommended for nausea, a must-have item.)
4. Mouthwash for sores in the mouth created by chemo.
5. A comedy CD - they will need it.
6. A meditation CD - they will want it.
7. Magazines - great for no-thinking kind of reading.
8. A journal to keep their ideas. It helps a lot during chemo brain.

According to cancer.org, chemo brain (also known as chemo fog or chemotherapy-related cognitive impairment and cognitive dysfunction) is real. Whatever you decide to call it, it can simply be defined as a lack of mental sharpness. It is frustrating for the patient and caregiver. During my research on cancer.net I found that the effects of chemo brain are usually short term, though chemo brain can occur in up to 75% of patients receiving chemo or radiation treatment. I found this shirt amusing as I was battling through "one of those days" of cancer. **"I have Chemo brain, what's your excuse?** "or another good one I found on Pinterest.

mY
bRAiN
iS
eXPeRIENcINg
tEChNiCAl
dIFFiCulTieS

pLEaSE
stAnd
By...

9. Notebook to keep ideas, directions, and medications organized.
10. Stationary to help pass the time because they may want to write to a friend, and it will be handy if electronic devices are not allowed. I wrote a lot of thank you cards during my chemotherapy sessions. A great idea is to include stamped envelopes with the persons return address. It will save them a trip to the post office and it will be a nice touch to show how much you care.
11. Facial tissue.
12. Tickets to an event eight months from when they started chemo. It gives them something to anticipate.
13. Slippers.
14. You could send them a card or letter in the mail. I still have many of the cards that were sent to me by my aunts who had gone through cancer or from friends showing support.

Everyone needs food:
15. Buy gift cards for take-out or delivery restaurants, then the family can use the cards when it is convenient.
16. Make frozen meals for the family
17. Even dropping off simple everyday groceries like milk, eggs, bread, and cereal can be helpful.

Cleaning, though it isn't important, is something that can get away from the family who is always running back and forth to the hospital. It's nice to come home from a day of doctor's appointments and have a corner of the couch that isn't covered in clothes. Depending on how well you know the family, this is something you can step in and do yourself, or there may be a company who will clean homes while the patient is undergoing treatment. Check out cleaningforareason.org or buy a gift certificate for a local cleaning company and let the family decide what time and service will work best for them. As I said, a clean house is not the most important thing, but it is a daily chore we all want done and this allows you to be able to help in a small way. Simply tell the family, "I have a cleaning service coming Tuesday while you are at treatment."

I realize earning the lawn of the month award is not crucial either. However, there was self-inflicted pressure for our lawn to be the same as it was when I was healthy. I don't know why; there just was. We didn't want there to be any sign we weren't handling everything perfectly. We had been juggling life and now there was a chainsaw, a flaming torch, and a bowling ball thrown into the mix, and we were determined to show the world we had talent! We were going to pull off this routine come hell or high water. If you know a family like us, you can mow, prune, plant or shovel snow for them. You could also hire someone to do these jobs for the family. You may think focusing on this is asinine. Honestly, life continues with or without the pruning of a lawn, but at the end of the day we all want to be comfortable. We want to keep our sense of normalcy. In the moments of life when things are spinning out of control it brings the human mind comfort to be able to prove we can hold some things together. We all prefer the laundry to be done, the sidewalk cleared, and dinner on the stove. When we can do just one of those things it keeps us from completely falling apart. Staying afloat becomes very hard when someone is thrown into the deep end of cancer. If you can take care of even one of the everyday mundane tasks for the family, it will mean they don't have to worry. It is worth it for you to focus on this insignificant task for them, because it will delay the "last straw" feeling for them. These are just a few ways you can help these families. Other great gift ideas to think about giving the self-reliant family:

18. A gas card, because the miles rack up quickly while running to appointments.
19. The gift of a car wash / detail – a luxury everyone enjoys.

20. Clothing gift cards to their favorite stores. The cancer patient may not want to be out in the crowd due to a low white blood cell count and fear of infection. That doesn't mean they won't want to do holiday or birthday shopping for their children.
21. Flowers - they are just sweet.
22. If the patient is receiving care far from home, giving some of your own hotel points will help them save money on lodging.

Then on a slightly different note, I have interviewed and compiled this handy dandy list of comfort items for caregivers. Some of these are great for the patient as well.

1. Possible membership to a gym. Remember caregivers need to take care of themselves. I suggest going with them or getting buddy passes from your own gym. This helps them to feel the comfort of a friend and they will make the time to go do this for themselves. This allows a time and place to de-stress. Caregivers will not do this on their own and will need you to encourage them to take some time for themselves.
2. Gift cards for coffee.
3. Gift cards for a meal. When you have been at the hospital all day it's nice to not have to worry about what you will plan to eat.
4. A massage gift card.
5. A manicure: this is a great opportunity to take your friend out and give them some down time. Some alone time. Some much needed "me" time. Caregivers need to stay strong while they are in front of the patient. Allow them some time to vent and crumble with you with no judgment: just a completely safe zone.
6. If a caregiver is willing, I strongly suggest doing something off the normal path. Go do an activity that is utterly ridiculous. None of the following adventures are

ridiculous any other time, but they may feel like the last practical thing they should be doing at that time. That is the point. Caregivers need to remember they don't always need to be practical. Go to a painting class, kayaking, rock climbing, or visit a trampoline event center. Do an activity that allows them to stick their tongues out at the world. By doing something a little immature they get a slightly freer perspective than they have had in a long time. This will allow them to take a deep breath and experience some relaxation.

7. A bottle of wine or favorite intoxicant.
8. Magazines, puzzle books, and inspirational reading for the long hours at the hospital.
9. Snacks or a stash of small dollar bills for the vending machines.
10. Relaxing music on CD.
11. Essential oils are very popular now and have been shown to help significantly with stress, depression, appetite, and immune support.

**Chapter 14: Here is the wind up, and the pitch…curve ball.**

October 2006: This is where my journal writing ended.

It was almost Halloween. I was getting really tired of my now "normal" routine. I was very worn down and the last few weeks of my journal were full of complaints about feverish nights. When I brought this up to the nurse, I was told it was normal. I was going through a lot of hormonal changes due to the pregnancy and oophorectomy, so that explanation made sense. I went along with their answer and tried to see this as something that I just needed to accept. At night, though, I would toss and turn and wake up covered in sweat and change my pajamas and pillowcase two or three times. I remember wandering through the house with insomnia and experiencing moments where my mind and body were going at different speeds. It felt like my thoughts were on fast-forward like a record on the wrong speed, while my body was moving slower than usual. I was informed I was experiencing chemo brain. Again, I felt reassured because people had a name for the things I was experiencing.

Lesson #77 learned: Just because people can put a name to what you are experiencing doesn't mean they are right or that it should make you feel better. My night sweats were made logical, but no one made them go away. My delusions had a name, but I felt like I was the only resident of Crazy Town.

It was during these increasingly hard times when I tried something I had learned in high school. I was told to pray about a subject and then pick up the Bible and randomly find a page. I will have to admit most of the time I have not found any *aha* moments when trying this little exercise. The upside was I always got distracted reading and found peace from the words. This time was different. This time I opened the Bible and turned right to Jeremiah 29:11. This would become my lifeline and the first Bible verse that I felt inspired to memorize.

*For I know well the plans I have in mind for you;*
*plans for your welfare and not for woe,*
*so as to give you a future of hope.*

It jumped off the page and I found myself reading it over and over again. There was hope.

Pete drove me to almost all my treatments. Something had come up though this late October day that allowed a friend to drive me to my chemotherapy. I had no idea at the time I was walking into my last day of treatment. I was feeling weaker than any other time during treatment. I would take the stairs one at a time and would feel exhausted after crossing the room. I was a sight, or what they call a *hot mess* in the South. Not anything about me resembled the healthy 28-year-old from just six weeks earlier. With some help, which seemed to gnaw away at my disappearing ego, I was escorted to the car and taken to the hospital. Instead of running me through the typical treatment, some vitals were taken instead. It was decided that I should be admitted and get some things checked out. Nurses could tell something was not right. This was more than chemo brain.

I stayed in the hospital overnight and consequently would miss my baby's first Halloween. It was a lonely and a draining stay, one of many I experienced that year. I was always in a fog, and there are really only two things I remember from the hospital stay. The first was that some med students performed an incredibly painful procedure called arterial blood sampling.

This is where a sample of blood is collected from an artery instead of my vein. The doctors wanted to see the gas composition of my blood. It hurt like hell. I could have sworn the students had made me their own voodoo doll. There were several attempts on my bony inner wrist. After they were done I curled into a ball and went to the only place of peace: slumber.

The other moment I remember from that stay was when Dr. Samir and his assistant checked on me and reported I would no longer need to do chemotherapy. I was off the hook and would not finish the last two weeks. It was determined chemotherapy was too hard on my body, and in essence, not worth it. You would imagine this news was the spiritual boost I needed, that I immediately felt relief and was overcome by immense joy. On the contrary, I only nodded my head and sat there unmoved and blank-faced. Dr. Samir even asked me if I had heard what he had said. I said "yep" and quickly faked a smile because I knew he was expecting a livelier reaction.

Physically, I reacted to the news less than half-heartedly, and emotionally my reaction was immeasurable. It was during this visit to the hospital I felt a switch had sprung in my mind. A sudden emotional disconnect. The sweats continued, and the racing thoughts haunted my days. Had I been sitting here five minutes or two hours? I had never experienced this feeling. I was disconnected from my baby and feeling like I was going mad. I was never comfortable, and I was jittery and unfocused.

Only days after being released from the hospital, I had turned into a robot and was completely emotionless. The world had changed, and I went from needing the time with my infant daughter to having a blasé attitude. *I. just. didn't. care.* I had checked out and was a shell of a person. I had to rely on Pete's memories of this time, as I can't recall any details. He could tell there was an emptiness behind my eyes and knew Stacey was in there but was slipping away. It was at this time he reached out to Dr. Samir for advice and a referral to a psychiatrist. Also, unbeknownst to me he had called my parents. He explained to them that I was not myself and he felt I was going to need more one-on-one care. Mom and Dad agreed to drive and pick up Faith so she could also get more one-on-one time.

With the quick phone call from Dr. Samir I was able to get into the psychiatrist the same afternoon. We can call this new villain Lucifer. Lucifer did see me just hours after we made the call, but made sure I was aware it was a personal favor to Dr. Samir and a huge benefit for me. He spoke with me for five minutes. He asked if I wanted to hurt myself and when I said, in a nutshell, "I really couldn't care less about anything," he left to speak with Pete in the hall right outside the office door. I sat there agitated; mind on permanent fast-forward and *alone*. I'm no doctor, but I would think there is a book somewhere that implies or specifically says, "Don't leave patients who are feeling hopeless by themselves and go within ear shot to talk about them." (I could be wrong, though.) So, if there wasn't a book that said it before, *there is one now!*

I could hear his judgments and condescension, which only made me angry. I decided I had been pushed far enough and, *dang it*, I was not going to be treated like a child. If dealing with Satan's Spawn had taught me anything, it was that I wasn't going to take this kind of treatment from anyone. If there is something going on, then tell *me*, the patient, *not* my husband. I started to boil over. I propelled myself out of the chair, went to the doorway, fixed my eyes on this pompous quack and said, "Are you going to tell *me* any of this?" Pete had the *oh shit* look and Lucifer was a bit startled I was in his face. I was told the game plan was to admit me to the hospital and get a head scan. I can assure you this isn't the first time in my life someone wanted to suggest this, but this man actually could order one.

By the time we were done and were ready to check into the hospital, my parents had arrived to take Faith. I was very surprised they were in the parking lot. I had no idea they had been called or that they were going to be taking my girl. Pete and my mom got busy rearranging the truck, loading the car seat and all of the baby items. My mom gave my dad specific directions to take care of me, and I just stood there holding my dad and he held me. This moment came from such an ugly time, but created such a beautiful moment. My dad just stood and held me, supported me. We didn't say anything; I was just held. I can't think of any moment with my dad that was as perfect. This moment may not seem miraculous to anyone else, but anyone who has met my strong and silent father will know this was *huge*.

Looking back at this particular chapter of my fight, I almost feel physically ill. I was weak. I wasn't a good mom and I get mad at the fact my best teammate wasn't by my side during this next phase. Faith had been there from the beginning. During this next turn of events, I didn't even care if she was there, yet I became incredibly angry when she had been removed from my reach. There were many mixed emotions. I just knew she had been the reason I found the cancer, and she was the reason I was going to beat it.

We left to go to the hospital and again I don't remember a lot of details, but I do remember the head scan was incredibly creepy. I remember something looking like a swim cap with metal buttons on it. I felt as if I was in an old sci-fi movie, but was relieved in remembering this contraption strapped to my head would at least keep the aliens from knowing my thoughts.

The results from the test didn't come in right away, and the next conversation with Lucifer came the following morning. My brother was visiting me at the hospital and I was lying in bed. Lucifer walked in and asked me how I was doing, and I tentatively said "fiiiinne."

"Oh, that's great! No other thoughts like you had yesterday?"

"No, I'm fine."

"Well, that sounds a lot better than fine. That's great!"

"Yeah, I guess."

The whole time I was thinking, *Dude*, there *is* such a thing as client patient confidentiality, which I am pretty sure is being broken right now. How can you expect me to be completely honest with you about my inner thoughts and lack of excitement about life, while someone was in the room? In his arrogance, he felt just being under *his* care for twenty-four hours had somehow changed my view on life. He hadn't counseled me, he hadn't even diagnosed a problem, and the total time he even had talked to me was ten minutes. He then went on to tell me he had made a special trip back just to see me. He had been an hour and a half away and came back to see how I was doing. *Really?* An hour and a half? You have got to be kidding me! He was doing his job and wanted me to grovel.

Needless to say, I never saw the man again; he is what people in my close circle call a DB (douche bag)! I wasn't healed just by being under his care. I was still having the same struggles, but could not go into any of my feelings while my brother sat there.

When the results came back, it was determined the port-a-cath in my chest used to administer my chemotherapy drugs, had created a blood clot in my internal jugular vein. This is a vein in one's neck responsible for draining blood from the head, brain, face and neck and bringing it towards the heart. Having the port-a-cath use a larger vein like the jugular vein allows the chemotherapy medications to immediately mix and dilute with a large volume of blood. When corrosive chemotherapy meds are given in smaller veins, the veins collapse.

This clot in the vein is called thrombosis and isn't incredibly rare. Protocol suggests removing the port and going on blood thinner for a short amount of time. Easy peasy, right? Well, let's fast forward this *particular* situation to a few months after getting off the blood thinners. I found out I still have the clot.

Fast forward even more where I'm ten years out from diagnosis: I have the clot and suffer from dizziness, especially when I bend over and all the blood rushes to my head. Unfortunately, this condition has not gotten me out of bending over to load the dishwasher or unload the dryer. Nor has it changed my role when it comes to gardening, tying shoes, cleaning up messes on my hands and knees or any of the other reasons we all find ourselves inverted on a daily basis. I deal with it and on more than one occasion, I just lean against a wall like a wino until I regain my balance.

Every two years I go in and have a cardiologist take a peak to see what the blood clot is doing. On my last trip, I was again reassured things were fine. On these trips, I am reminded that the human body is an amazing machine. At a glance of me in a tank top you can physically see the veins of my upper torso rerouting around this little blockage. I say little because the vessel I am told is around 2cm in diameter. In all actuality, the clot blocks more than 90% of the vessel so though it is a 2cm freeway from my head to my heart pretty much all lanes are closed and will be for the rest of my life. Doctors are not concerned about the clot dislodging so I guess I shouldn't be either, right? The blockage hasn't increased and my dizzy spells really aren't any worse than they were when this all started. The coolest thing about this clot is seeing the live images of blood making new pathways and just going around it. Every time I see it I am amazed at what our bodies can do.

Problem number two of this leg of the race is while I was in the hospital I found out I was low in magnesium. I don't know of too many people who could tell you why we need magnesium. Or what the chemical symbol is? Or where we would find it in our daily diet? I can now tell you it is needed for more than 300 biochemical reactions in the body. It helps to maintain normal nerve and muscle function, cuts your risk of heart attacks, and supports a healthy immune system, while warding off depression (among other things). Its symbol is Mg, and can be found in dark leafy greens, seeds and nuts, fish, soybeans, avocados, bananas, dark chocolate and low-fat yogurt, just in case you are playing any trivia games! Now that we have this simple diagnosis we can see I wasn't completely insane.

The feelings of hopelessness, the depression and loss of time was being identified and diagnosed. I now had medical proof and it had a name: I was suffering from hypomagnesaemia. That would have been enough to make the hospital stay worthwhile, but we also found yet another problem.

Problem number three while on this long hospital stay: I encountered yet another nemesis. This opponent goes by the formal name of Transient Ischemic Attack (TIA). This is when blood flow to part of the brain stops for a short period of time. It's like mini stroke. A third of the time a TIA will precede a true stroke. The symptoms of TIA are similar to a full-blown stroke, and they are both caused by clots. The difference is when a TIA occurs the clot is just stuck for a second and moves on. TIA's don't last long, usually no longer than five minutes and usually TIA's do not create long-term effects. Besides the clot we know about in my jugular vein, there must have been another that caused the TIA. I knew there was something wrong when I had numbness and was having trouble recalling words. My cognition was tested and it was determined that night I had indeed experienced a TIA. It was the oddest feeling of being shown a picture of an everyday item and having your brain search for material you know has been stored away. It's your mind fighting with itself to hurry up and answer the questions you would typically answer in a fraction of a second.

"Mrs. Peterson, can you tell me what this is a picture of?"

"Sure........."
      (My internal dialogue ensues)

"Hurry up and tell the nice nurse what it is!"

"Shut up, I'm trying. "

"You two stop fighting and answer the question. They are timing this!"

"Right, as if I didn't already know that. You standing there yelling at me to *go faster* isn't going to help the situation."

"Ya know, he is right! If you really want to be helpful, you'd tell us what the picture is!"

"Of course, I will have to save the day *again*. Anyone knows, **that** is a picture of a ... well, you know the thing you put on your ... Um that, ah... It starts with a 's' and it ya know ties. (pause) Shoe! Yes, say the word shoe. Go ahead, you remember how to form that word. Say shoe. Final answer!"

Me: "Shoe"

Nurse: "Okay next picture."

Ugh...I was having a scene from the movie *Inside Out* played out in my head ten years before the movie debuted! There was more internal struggling and confusion as I was tested with more cards.

If this were a comic strip, you would read the words "meanwhile back at the ranch..." Our beautiful little girl was staying with grandma and papa and our lives were running parallel, not connected in any way.

Mid way through my stay at the hospital my favorite uncle called me to check-in with me. It is very common during our conversations for a lot of sarcasm, laughing and love. He is the grandson of ornery Granny Lizzy, so we get along well. We didn't talk long because this conversation was not like anything we had shared before. There was forced laughter by me, short answers, and I remember trying to fake the happiness. He wasn't fooled, and he called my parents shortly after we hung up to check and see if he needed to drive the over six hundred miles to get me shaped up. They told him no, but he was determined to send me inspiration in the mail and show his love every way he knew how. He wasn't going to leave me hanging, and he did what he felt the situation warranted; orneriness at its best, and at that…from afar. He didn't let me push him away and made sure to make follow up calls and send mail.

I knew when I was getting better because the pull to be with my baby girl was stronger, and the joy of being a mom was telling me to go hold her. Being away from our daughter had created another terrible glitch that medicine couldn't fix. I was losing those mom moments, the baths, the late-night feedings, the rocking her to sleep. Those are the moments when you really connect to a baby. When I finally did get to hold my girl, she didn't know me. I wasn't strong enough to bounce the way she liked while standing because I was just too tired. Even though I was now physically with her, I felt useless. She didn't want me.

Let me stop for a moment and tell you something about our girl. Although she had come into this world small at four pounds and one ounce, she never slowed down. If you have had the pleasure of meeting our firecracker, you will agree in ten years she has not taken a day off. The kid runs a hundred miles an hour for twelve straight hours and when forced to be horizontal she sleeps harder than anyone I know. (I am so jealous.) There was a study done once about Olympic athletes being challenged to do adult versions of what toddlers do daily and the toddlers won the endurance test. The professionals were no match, and now you can understand why parents are so tired. We have not been training long enough to handle these marvels. Somehow Faith has been able to bottle this endurance and still runs circles around people even today. Faith doesn't understand the concept of slowing down or sitting out of playtime. I helped coach her fast pitch softball team, and I was once again reminded of her genetic orneriness and her feelings to constantly challenge the universe. At one of her softball games when she was seven, she was asked to take her turn and sit on the bench for an inning. All the kids needed to at some point in the season, and her number had come up. With a heavy heart and much disappointment, she plopped her small frame next to me on the bench. I gave her the tough love speech and she turned to me and said, "I didn't come here to sit on the bench!" THIS is what I deal with on a daily basis. Though it is a challenge sometimes, as her mother I try to remind myself it is this same spirit that willed her to grow and move mountains as a baby and that same spirit will carry her on to amazing things throughout her whole life. (Consider this your warning!)

She is a child who grandparents love to see. I say that because she challenges me daily in the ways I can't explain. Most parents won't appreciate these challenges; grandparents on the other hand enjoy watching their own child figuratively pull her hair out in frustration over the mental hurdles their grandchild has created. Their wish has come true; I got a child that acts the way I once did.

I can remember the first time my eyes were opened to what my baby had in her. After my c-section I stayed in the hospital for a few days. I was busy running to different scans and completing testing that couldn't be done while I was pregnant. After we got our snuggles in the NICU, Pete would take me to my own appointments. Then we would rush back to see our pink bundle. On one occasion after scrubbing up and donning the correct protective apparel, I peeked my head into Faith's room. Her nurse was just finishing up some paperwork before she moved on to the next baby. I cautiously asked how Faith was doing. The nurse was real serious and in a hushed tone leaned in to whisper, "Shhhh, don't tell her she is small. She doesn't know." What a concept. If we don't know the situation is supposed to be a challenge, then our mind and body go on to amaze the world. Faith's little body didn't know that she was supposed to be struggling. She didn't know that 'this' wasn't normal. She was simply channeling her Great Grandmother and being ornery. In her own way, she was saying "I GOT THIS! I just want to go home to my new nursery and get all these machines off me." Let me tell you, she has continued to say those words throughout her short life. "Stand back, I got this. Let me shine!"

We had been told our baby would stay in the hospital for eight weeks, until her original due date. This is a typical answer for any premature baby. But, no sir! This baby, after only sixteen DAYS was ready to come home. This was a shock to us. We did not expect for them to tell us she was going to be coming home. In fact, mom guilt slapped me in the face hard again, because when they told me she could come home September 11, 2006, I had to ask if she could please stay one more day. You see, I was scheduled to have my port and first chemo appointment and was not ready to take all this on. Like many first-time moms, I wasn't sure I was ready for this little human, especially since I was only firing on about half my pistons. The nurses looked shocked at my request. "I had no idea. Of course she can stay!"

During the following days, weeks, and months, my daughter would outshine me. I read a sign recently: "It's not my fault that when I was baby I was dropped in glitter." That is our Faith. At least in this mom's eyes, she has stepped into this world shining and people can't help but be entranced by the shimmer. She is fun and full of excitement. She has so many questions and wants to try everything. If she wasn't my daughter, I might not like her much because of my jealous nature. She's one of those people you want to be like, but they almost make you pull your hair out because they do everything with such ease. She is truly blessed.

I didn't always feel this motherly overindulgence. During those terrible days in the hospital working through the blood infection, blood clot, and TIA, I was not myself and was disconnected from the world. I can honestly say all this other junk was harder on me than the cancer, or at least it felt like it was the knockout punch.

In early November when I was admitted to the hospital and given all the brain scans, waiting to hear my prognosis was really a tough time for me. Not knowing for sure what my opponent was, challenged me greatly. Then the unclear idea of what to do next to help regulate my blood levels was finally too much for me to handle. It was the last straw for me. I had given up and I did not feel like the doctors were helping me. I felt unbalanced and very alone. My body had been weak for a long time, but when a person's mental and spiritual state becomes weak, then you really have a problem.

If the voices in your head are all you are left with and they become negative, the body is bound to follow them. I would venture to say everyone who has ever experienced major medical experiences has had a bout of depression and woe. The difference is how far each person goes into the depression and the feelings of hopelessness, plus the duration they stay there. It is crucial, in my opinion, to have a figurative life vest close at hand. Maybe it will be your pastor, a friend, or counselor. There were people around to help me, but I didn't feel comfortable reaching out to anyone to tell them what was going on in my head. I didn't want to show another weakness. I didn't want to share something I figured no one else would be feeling or would be able to understand. Again, if I would have been strong enough to seek out a support group, I may have found answers. I was often in a room full of people, and yet felt very alone. I smiled to make sure others weren't left feeling uncomfortable with the situation. I was losing hope that there would ever be an answer or a bright day again. It was hard to be real with anyone, and to bear my true thoughts and feelings.

The options of how you will regain your mental strength are endless. You may not be ready to physically talk with professionals or survivors. Maybe a book or movie could help you regain focus. Some people found their strength in Rhonda Byrne's book, *The Secret*, which was widely popular the year I was diagnosed. I will be honest; every time I sat down to watch the movie based on this book I would fall asleep. I was exhausted from the chaos in my life and I could never stay focused on the movie long enough for it to help me in any other way than as a sleeping aid. I have honestly tried a visual board, but it just wasn't for me. It just felt too much like "if you build it, they will come." Good philosophy, but not something to really help me focus.

Caregivers, it may be a challenge to identify when a patient has reached *that* moment when they are ready to crumble. So first, I would suggest simple forms of showing love, sympathy, and support to help combat their feelings. Two, silence. This allows words to flow freely from the inside struggles the patient is feeling. You will need to be strong to handle what is really bothering them.

I guess these last ramblings can be best summarized by simply saying *just love the person* who is struggling and be whatever it is *they* need. Sometimes I needed the proverbial kick in the butt; sometimes I needed a good cry; and other days I would be able to take on a prizefighter with my words. There will be many ups and downs, and it is hard for any one person to be all these supporters to the patient. Patients, surround yourself with as many people as you can who will easily take on these different roles. We all possess specific and natural talents. A catcher is not a centerfielder, and a first baseman is not a short stop. Make sure to equip your team with a variety of people and don't be afraid to bench a few players who don't see today's game plan. I encourage you to sit for a moment and think of the people who are close to you. What are their gifts? Who will be the person who verbally supports you, prays with you, and loves on your beautiful soul? Who will be the one who tells you to get off your butt and walk around the block with you? Who will just sit and watch TV with you? This trip is hard and the roller coaster of emotions that you will feel is normal. Try your best to equip yourself with the strongest team possible early on.

*1 Corinthians 12: 27-29*
*All of you together are Christ's body, and each of you is a part of it. Here are some of the parts God has appointed for the church: first are apostles, second are prophets, third are teachers, then those who do miracles, those who have the gift of healing, those who can help others, those who have the gift of leadership, those who speak in unknown languages. Are we all apostles? Are we all prophets? Are we all teachers? Do we all have the power to do miracles? Do we all have the gift of healing? Do we all have the ability to speak in unknown languages? Do we all have the ability to interpret unknown languages?*

Of course not! One person cannot do everything, but many people, if you let them, can. Allow others to use their gifts and collectively you can fight this battle.

**Chapter 15: Things not to say to a cancer patient.**

I feel after having this experience with cancer I can honestly declare: people say really dumb things. I found out it isn't obvious to everyone that sometimes saying nothing is exactly the perfect thing to say. One of my favorite sayings is from a Greek philosopher Epictetus: *"We have two ears and one mouth so we can listen twice as much as we speak."* Cancer patients may just want to talk. To vent. To purge their feelings. Other times they are too tired to put their feelings into words and at that point hearing a random antidote is perfect. Not your work issues or simple complaints, because when you sit and complain to them it is hard for them not to think, *I had poison drilled into my body today.* Trust me, their story will trump yours every time, and it should. Lastly, silence isn't all bad. Just be content to sit. Hold their hand. Pray. Nothing has to be said, especially if it's inconsiderate, rude, needs to be explained, or is plain stupid. I have compiled my top six things not to say to a cancer patient, but if you ask any cancer patient they will have their own.

1.   **"You look like Brian Urlacher!"** Now, I know this first one seems extremely obvious. No woman ever wants to be compared to a NFL linebacker, ever. To say this phrase to a woman who is hopped up on steroids from her cancer treatment, who is hormonal due to post-partum, depressed due to a cancer diagnosis, and bald due to chemotherapy, is truly putting your life in your own hands. Maybe this statement works on guys who are in treatment; I'm not sure. It is safe to say though: it is *never* okay to say this to a woman, *ever.* I will go one step farther, just in case you are confused and think it is only linebackers we don't want to be compared to. Rest assured, don't ever make physical comparisons between a woman and *any* football player. *Nay, any male athlete.* Nope. male, *period.* (Reflection: this is different than

me using imagery in chapter 11 and comparing my own moves to a NFL running back.)

2. If I had enforced rule number one early on, then this second statement would have never been made. **"You look like your brother!"** Really? That's what you are going to go with the first time you see me in my hospital bed? *Wow!* Staying clear of making any comments on my general appearance while I am in the hospital or going through treatment would be appreciated. There are few people who can actually pull off a genuine comment, so amateurs beware. "You look …good." The eyes give it away every time. The sad eyes of hurt, pain, uncomfortableness, and pity are hard to hide. I know I look like crap, and it only makes sense because I feel like crap, too. Let's just refrain from commenting on my outward appearance.

3. **"Wow, you remind me of GI Jane."** Though Demi portrays a strong, capable, physical specimen in this movie, this statement is only slightly higher to the first no-no comment. This is mostly because of the gender, and secondly because of how amazing a Navy Seal is. In my experience, though, women don't want their bald head to be the focus of any conversation.

4. **"Your wig looks great."** Really? If it did, you wouldn't know it was a wig! Refraining from saying anything is okay in my book.

5. **"You look tired."** Gee, I wonder why? Please don't tell someone they look tired. Their body is being attacked by chemicals. Doctors will get you as close to death just so they can save you. No kidding. I think *chemo* means *torture* in Swahili. Telling me I look tired when I *am* tired will make me cranky. Telling me I look tired when

I am actually having a good day will make me cranky. Telling me that I'm cranky and not myself will get you punched in the throat! My advice: *don't go there.*

6. Here's my last point, and yes, a person actually told me this. **"Your cancer really isn't that bad."** They had no medical degree and they hadn't even stayed at a Holiday Inn the night before. They just felt the need to throw their random thoughts at me. No warning, nothing. Just felt like they should share their thoughts of my cancer not being "that bad." After ten years, I still don't understand this statement. I do understand there are types of cancers and stages of cancers that have better prognoses than others. I understand I was diagnosed early. However, someone standing on the outside perfectly healthy should not tell the sick bald woman she really doesn't have it too bad. Did you want to change spots then? No? Why?

I don't know if this list of what not to say was helpful or not, but I hope it at least makes you stop before you speak. So, what can you say to a patient? I know I am making this hard, aren't I? Know that patients are dealing with situations that seem unfathomable. That unless you have walked in their shoes you won't get it and even then, your situation was probably very different from theirs. Just be quiet and listen. This is an opportunity for you. Learn what is happening. Try to understand what they are feeling and going through. Things do happen for a reason and sometimes it's the bystanders who need the lesson.

For me, my bald head was something very hard for me to come to terms with, much harder than I ever expected. I never had been too girly, so I didn't think losing my hair would affect me so greatly. Here is what I figured out, though. *A woman's hair is tied directly to her identity.* Men can be bald and the world won't know for sure if it is a choice, genetics, or cancer. For women, the first assumption is cancer. When I started to lose my hair this all became very real. I could hide the scars. Makeup helped to give me an extra boost of color. No hair though, that was a tough one to explain. Friends and family had known I was sick, but now *everyone* knew. That was hard for me. I wanted to have control of telling people; instead there it was for all to see.

I just want the general reader to understand that by pointing out the obvious you are pouring salt in the wound. Please just be conscious of your words, thinking them through carefully and if you ever for a moment think, *this could be taken the wrong way*, then for goodness sake, don't say it!

> *"Give me a head with hair, long beautiful hair*
> *Shining, gleaming, streaming, flaxen, waxen*
> *Give me down to there, hair, shoulder length or*
> *longer. Here baby, there, momma, everywhere,*
> *daddy, daddy"*
> ~*Musical: Hair*

I had told myself I wasn't ever going to wear a scarf. Wearing a scarf would make me feel like there was a bull's-eye painted on me and I was bound and determined to blend in. I was going to be okay with all this because I had a plan to avoid it. I was fortunate enough to be set up with a foundation in my community that would get me a free high-quality wig, as beautiful as a wig can get. The wig I had gotten was the same hairstyle as my own, and the same color, too. This trip to get my wig was made painless by a gal who had been through this situation herself. At this point, Jean was "just a coworker," a woman I knew. I volunteered with her for our town's largest run/walk to raise money for cancer. We worked at the same fitness center but our paths rarely crossed. I was just a little older than her own children, and we didn't have a lot in common. When the news did get out that I had cancer, I remember even being confused as to why she had called me. We didn't know each other well, why was she planning to have meals brought to the house during treatment? Answer: *because there are angels among us.* Jean is an ornery woman, herself. That's why we get along well. She has beaten breast cancer and she continues to tackle everything life throws at her with gusto. She realized that going to get a wig was going to be worse than the fear women experience when trying on swimsuits in early spring. She made it so easy it was done before I knew it. She was positive and upbeat without being fake or goofy. I was still moving forward with a good amount of grace because at this point I didn't *need* the wig. I was just shopping, and the fact I was getting a wig and not a new pair of shoes was irrelevant. Jean's skill, Del (the woman who helped us), and my wild imagination and delusion were a great combination.

September 25, 2006: I had been told the fourteenth day after treatment started would be significant. That day would mark the day my hair would start to fall out. Right on schedule it did. I noticed it first with my pubic hair, which was a real shocker, as no one thinks about the pubic hair. Then I noticed how bad my hair hurt on my head. I know you will tell me my hair couldn't hurt, but I say *nay nay*. (Thank you to the late John Pinnette for the perfect alliteration.) My hair truly *hurt*! To even lift or move it away from my face felt like I was lifting frozen leather and it was going to snap at the roots at any moment. I told Pete in passing this terrible event had started and I just wanted him to have a heads up. I was totally trying to play it cool. Two days later my hair was all over the place. I had decided I must take this situation into my own hands. Pete volunteered to shave my head. I should have reached out to someone to talk to when this was all happening. I was trying to be okay with it and take it on the chin, but honestly, it was hard. As all the dark hair fell around me I cried and tried to remember it was just hair, and it would come back. Rationality doesn't solve everything. I had Pete cover the bathroom mirror as I wasn't ready to look at myself. I wouldn't be ready for twenty-four hours to look in the mirror. I knew that reality would be staring back at me from the mirror. No hiding it or denying it. I wasn't ready, and now everyone was going to know.

I had cancer.

On the upside though I will say not having hair is very cooling and laying a bald head on a satin pillow is heavenly. Also, the amount of time it takes to get ready in the morning drops to a total of ten minutes. Total!

I had hair on Friday when I went to my treatment and then on Monday when I returned I was rocking my wig, or so I thought. I had convinced myself it looked natural. First the doctor points it out (jab), and then the chemo nurse (upper cut). What? I wasn't fooling anyone? Then why was I wearing it? The statements weren't hurtful per se, but if people could tell I was wearing a wig then what was the point?

This hair moment was soul shaking. Five of my six rules mentioned earlier in this chapter pertain to losing my hair. Losing my hair along with the steroids created more masculine biased features. Hair loss exaggerated my genetics as well as made me look a little worn out. Losing my hair struck me hard and I feel most women and kids will have similar responses. As I said before, a bald man can roll rather naturally through life and people won't know for sure. Women and children are supposed to have hair; otherwise people ask questions.

*"Manners are a sensitive awareness of the feelings of others. If you have that awareness, you have good manners, no matter what fork you use."*
~ Emily Post

## Chapter 16: A Perfect Song List for This Cancer Patient

When I think back to any important part of my life I immediately think of the soundtrack I was creating to go with it. Some of my first memories were listening to silly songs like "Kookie Kookie Lend me your Comb" by Edd Byrnes, "Charlie Brown, He's a Clown" by the Coasters, and "Beep Beep, The Little Nash Rambler" by the Playmates on the ol' turn table. I soon progressed to eight tracks and found Mac Davis, The Oak Ridge Boys, the Footloose soundtrack and Supertramp. It wasn't till writing this book that I even knew what the actual words were to "It's Raining Again." Our daughter's love of music is growing and I swear she has a new favorite song every couple of months. "Mom, you gotta listen to this! It's *awesome!*" So, the tradition continues, music is braided into our lives.

I was just a little older than she is now when I was jamming out to Debbie Gibson, and Young Mc on my boom box, while I used a pencil to thread the tape back into my Weird Al Yankovic and Milli Vanilli cassettes. Popping on the headphones of my sisters Walkman I'd listen to all the songs I had patiently recorded each Sunday from the radios top 40 countdown. This kept me occupied for most of my junior high life.

I'm sure when you think of your junior high dances, homecoming, college parties, road trips, and the first song you danced to as husband and wife you are transported back. You can't help but smile. Music has a way of bringing sparkle to our lives. We really do create soundtracks for our lives, and by looking at how diverse mine was as a kid you will be able to appreciate that my assorted playlist still sweeps many genres to match my mood.

Music is beautiful and has such immense powers. Whether I am using it to get pumped up to take on a work out or to slow myself down and get a much-needed rest, I am surrounded by music. The words get stuck on repeat in our heads. The beat consumes us and we can't help but get our Night at the Roxbury head bob on, even when we have no clue to the correct lyrics.

I have tried to compile a list for you to check out over the next few weeks. Each song has strong meaning and purpose. These diverse songs serve as the speeches you will need throughout your journey. Remember when I told you that there is a need for different people in your circle to tell you to "Shape up!" or "I'm here for you." Well, these songs do just that. They give support, tough love and everything in between.

1. "Beautiful Day" (U2). It worked for Congresswoman Gabrielle Gifford!

2. "Better Days" (The Goo Goo Dolls). This one still makes me cry.
My favorite lines from this song are:
*And you asked me what I want this year,*
*And I try to make this kind and clear*
*Just a chance that maybe we'll find better days,*
*'Cause I don't need boxes wrapped in strings.*
*And designer love and empty things,*
*Just a chance that maybe we'll find better days.*

It just seemed to put things into perspective. I didn't want stuff. I wanted to feel better, I wanted things to slow down and return to my normal.

3. "Diamonds" (Hawk Nelson)
4. "Fight Song" (Rachel Platten). I always feel inspired by this song.
5. "Fireworks" (Katy Perry). The lyrics are awesome. I just think we need to hear that we are amazing, brilliant,

breath-taking and so special. We are lucky to have YOUR brilliance in our life. Meaningful lines from this song include

> *"There is a spark in you!* and *Own the night like the Fourth of July!"*

6. "Going Through Hell" (Rodney Atkins). I wore this song out the first year.
7. "Happy" (Pharrell Williams). You'll need this one for lines like,

> *Can't let nothing bring me down.*

8. "Just Breathe" (Jonny Diaz). The chorus is perfect.

> *Breathe, just breathe.*
> *Come and rest at my feet. And be. Just be.*
> *Chaos calls but all you really need,*
> *Is to just breathe.*

9. "Home" (Blake Sheldon and Michael Buble). I like the Christmas version.
10. "Stronger (What Doesn't Kill You)" (Kelly Clarkson). Since treatment I've run many races, and this is the song that gets me over those hills.
11. "I'm Gonna to Love You Through it" (Martina McBride).
12. "I'm the Man" (Aloe Blacc).

> *"Somewhere I heard that life is a test. I've been through the worst and I still give my best."*

13. "Just be Held" (Casting Crowns). This first verse gets me every time. It won't matter what you are going through it will cause your eyes to burn and your vision to blur.

> *"Hold it all together, Everybody needs you strong. But life hits you out of nowhere, And barely leaves you holding on. And when you're tired of fighting, Chained by your control. There's freedom in surrender Lay it down and let it go. So, when you're on your knees and*

*answers seem so far away. You're not alone,
Stop holding on and just be held **Your world's
not falling apart, It's falling into place** I'm on
the throne, stop holding on and just be held. Just
be held, just be held"*

14. "Little Wonders" (Rob Thomas)
15. "Live Like You Were Dying" (The fabulous Tim McGraw). This song changed my life. Watch his performance on YouTube when he performs at Stand Up to Cancer. You won't be disappointed. By the way, I did go skydiving. I did hike in the Rockies. I rode a mechanical bull; I know it isn't quite the same but it's close enough. I've been reading more of the Bible. Went fishing with my dad and daughter. Loved deeper then I have ever before and fight to be the friend a friend would like to have.

*fishing with Papa

16. "My Daughter's Eyes" (Martina McBride). It got me up and helped me think how I wanted to get through this life. If you haven't heard this song, you have to listen to it.
17. "One Day You Will" (Lady Antebellum).
18. "Overcomer" (Mandisa)
19. "Praise You in This Storm" (Casting Crowns).
20. "Riser" (Dierks Bentley)

21. "Roar" (Katy Perry). This one is for when it's time to be ornery.
22. "Stand by You" (Rachel Platten). I dare you not to dance.
23. "The World's Greatest" (R. Kelly). This was recommended by Pete.
24. "This is My Story" (Big Daddy Weave). This one is for if you need an explanation to why there is so much of my faith reflected in this book.

    *O to tell you my story, is to tell of Him*
    *O to tell you my story, is to tell of Him*
    *This is my story, this is my song*
    *Praising my savior all the day long.*

25. "Trust in You" (Lauren Daigle).
26. "Tubthumping" (Chumbawumba) We all get knocked down, but we need to get up again. Besides, this brings me back to a carefree time that just makes me smile.
27. "You Gotta Be" (Des'ree). An oldie but a goodie.
28. "Tell Your Heart to Beat Again" (Danny Gokey).

    *You're shattered, like you've never been before.*
    *The life you knew in a thousand pieces on the*
    *floor. And words fall short in times like these*
    *When this world drives you to your knees*
    *You think you're never gonna get back, To the*
    *you that used to be.*

## Chapter 17: "You don't look like a cancer patient"

What does that even mean? Thanks, I guess.

I have been blessed to attend three national conferences concerning ovarian cancer. I was able to listen to some amazing stories. When I sat through the first two conferences I got my first inspiration to write my story. It was also my first opportunity to meet Diem Brown and hear her speak. There is something almost palpable in a room that is filled with men and women gathered for the same cause. Sure, there are tears, but there is so much positive power going in the right direction that you can't help but be swept up in the emotional current. The conferences help to educate participants on where the disease is currently, and what leaps science is making. I have been able to listen to speakers provide information about nutritional health, fashion, dental health, outer beauty and spiritual health, all focusing on the patient. The best part, without a doubt, is listening to women who have been there and done all of that! The one thing I see in all the authors and professional speakers who share their stories is the fire and passion for life. They are ornery! They have been knocked down, but they got back up again and are spreading the word that getting the diagnosis of cancer does not have to be a life sentence.

In 2014 there was a panel of five amazing women who were in all stages of remission sharing their ideas and stories about how they got through the roughest parts of their cancer journey. This was the highlight of the trip for many attendees. The stage was set up as something right off a television talk show. The panel sat in individual chairs each answering the same questions.

When the women were given the topic of deferring happiness, I feel they all responded with the same answer, but with their own special take on the matter. This was perfect as each speaker, I think, was speaking to different women in the audience. Each one of us seated in the ocean in front of them were nodding our heads as different woman on the panel nailed the verbiage for the attendees' particular inner voice. For some women, not deferring their happiness meant cancer had given them a "Get Out of Jail Free Card." Cancer had taken away any excuses that had been holding them back. For some, playing the cancer card had become the silver lining. This may sound unethical, but there will come a day in treatment as you stand in line, take a number or get served the wrong food that you will want to say…*I'm sorry, I just got through with my treatment for today. I'm nauseous and tired; would you mind if I went in front of you in line and bought just these two items.* We all have times when we want an easy button. Trust me, you deserve the cut in line, the free refill, or to be encouraged to merge into traffic.

Along those same lines another speaker put it as simply as "Just do what makes you happy." This idea can be tricky. I don't mean that you should take from your employer because you deserve it, or demand time and objects from your friends and family. Too many people these days feel they need to take their fair share from the world. The sense of entitlement is unnecessarily strong.

What I mean is that there is no one who deserves happiness more than the person who is fighting for his or her life. So, after days of diarrhea, if you want to have chocolate cake as your meal then I say *do it*! If you want to wear your pajamas all day, who is it going to hurt? Going through cancer is hard and if you can do something simple to make life bearable then, yes, I feel you should do it. Make yourself happy. Take those moments, though brief and fleeting, to stop and be happy doing something you enjoy. *You deserve it!*

During this miserable time, you will see so many blessings around you if you can simply stop. Maybe when there are little fingers grasping yours. Hugs, the good kind, from loved ones.

Cards from friend's miles away will show up in the mail and remind you that you are not alone and you are loved. I *still* have the cards I received from family who were too far away to physically visit me. There is beauty in your support team. *Find that beauty* and cling to it because there is so much ugly right now. This is one of the best gifts cancer gave me. As I mentioned I was diagnosed when I was 28 years old. I was working two jobs and playing sports three nights a week. I did not have a care in the world and had always lived a life that kept me racing against myself to see what could be done and how fast. I was not stopping to smell any roses.

Cancer helped me to find beauty. I would have eventually calmed down. I would have started enjoying sunrises, the sound of waves or the smell of rain, but cancer helped me realize the small things about thirty years earlier than most people. Cancer took a lot away, but it also gave me a lot. There is an understanding of life you can only get through experiences. I once got into a face-to-chest conversation with someone who wanted to tell me I didn't have enough years under my belt to have opinions, insight, or wisdom. I became ornery and looked up at this guy and told him it doesn't have as much to do with how many rings are on the tree as it does with how many storms the tree has weathered.

I look back at that confrontation and smirk that the conversation got me so riled up. Just because I don't look like a cancer survivor doesn't mean that I don't come into every conversation with a non-elective tattoo, a deep understanding of my faith and life, and a new degree of education given by the School of Hard Knocks. I am not special because of this. There are many in this same boat. There are many young trees learning to bend instead of break.

When I think back to the conference talks, I ask myself how I would have answered the panel questions. I think *my* answers

about deferring happiness would be yet another list. My answers
would be:
1. Balance
2. Live
3. Accept
4. *And make lists*

Having balance in our lives is important no matter your age or
situation. I just think it is extremely important during the cancer
journey that patients can give themselves a break. You have to
realize when you are going through this, you aren't going to feel
the way you usually do. You aren't going to be able to do what
you typically would do. *Balance life out and take a deep breath.*
Balance your day with what needs to get done and what you
want to get done. Find balance and don't push yourself too hard.
Finding emotional balance is just as important as finding
balance in your routine.

Live in a way that makes you feel alive. Do things you enjoy.
Do things that make you smile and don't be surprised that you
feel the best when you are helping someone else.

> *"... the surest way to be happy is to seek*
> *happiness for others."*
> *~ Martin Luther King Jr.*

Live in the moment. Live in a way you can be proud of. Live so
at the end of the day when you lay down to sleep, you take in a
deep breath, sigh and smile as you drift off knowing it was a
day well lived.

Accept that this is where you are at this moment. Accept that
you are exactly where you need to be. Accept that you have
what you need to handle this and accept that it will be all right.
There are only about five minutes per day that should be wasted
on the "could of, would of, should of's" that happen when you

throw a pity party. Hey, I'm being generous, and I will let you have those five minutes. Then, I want you to think about this saying from Colin Powell:

> *"Always focus on the front windshield and not the review mirror."*

Look forward and then move forward. You are still here. That means you aren't done. That means there is a reason. That means you need to take the bull by the horns, teach him who's boss, and then rest easy at the end of the day back on the porch as you look over a green pasture at sunset. I know not everyone wants to hear this or can accept this right now, but, God has got this. God has you in His healing hands and will get you through this detour. He will be there to carry you when you can't muster the energy and He will be there cheering you on as you finish the race.

*Proverbs 3:5-6*
*Trust in the LORD with all your heart, on your own intelligence do not rely; In all your ways be mindful of Him, and He will make straight your paths.*

Number four, on how to defer happiness: I must say *lists* because I would be making lists to make the other three happen. Make the lists that help create your *balanced* day. Write the list that provides you the direction to move forward and allows you to continue to live instead of getting bogged down in misery. It can be a wish list, a bucket list, or a to-do list. Lastly, making a list helps you accept who you are right now. A list of mantras helps you get up, get dressed, and make it through each moment.

1. *"Ok, let's do this!"*
2. *"Bring it."*
3. *"Everything is possible with God."*

4. *"Why not?"*
5. *"Don't suck!"*

Even making lists of doctor instructions will make the daunting task of living with cancer less overwhelming. When taken in these small bites we can accept life a little more easily.

> *"How do you eat an elephant? One bite at a time."*
> *~General Creighton Abrams*

Another question this particular speaking panel was asked concerned the consuming feeling patients have to apologize for everything during cancer treatment. *I am sorry you need to drive me to treatment. I am sorry I won't be able to keep my appointment/date with you; I am not feeling well. I am sorry I just don't feel like eating. Sorry, I am too tired.* This whole panel came back with a resounding *don't be apologetic!* It is okay to put yourself first. We need to understand that putting our health first is our main objective. Listen to what you need to do and try and muster the strength to do it. Give yourself a break, and understand that being emotional during this obviously difficult time is inevitable. Don't apologize for the fact that you have less patience, or that you are just having a bad day. Try to understand you will change not just physically through this journey, but emotionally you will grow into someone new as well. Accept this new you, and don't apologize if your metamorphosis has others feeling slightly uncomfortable. I challenge you to rephrase your comments. *Thank you for being patient; I'm moving a little slowly this morning. Thank you for bringing me to treatment; the company is a great change. Thank you for the invite; can we do Friday instead?*
Caregivers and the supporting actors in your life may feel discomfort over your cancer. That discomfort will go away, but you will still have cancer. There isn't an option for you to just step away from cancer but, some people will choose to step

away from you until life is back to normal. Also, it is inexcusable for others to come into your screenplay and try to direct you and all that is happening. I know most of these people mean well and don't understand what they are doing, but it doesn't make it okay. As for me, I found myself answering this forum question in my head with a saying I use a lot...*This isn't about you!*

Please understand I am extremely grateful for the help and support I received during my diagnosis and treatment. So, when I say, "this isn't about you," it is simply a way for me to put things into perspective. I even use it on myself sometimes.

Some people will change the situation into their own story of how cancer is impacting them, and that their life is consumed with cancer. Don't be that person. Remember it's the patient's life that is being consumed by cancer. Who did they cut into? Who lost their hair? Who almost died? Who is sitting alone because it is too hard for bystanders to make it to the hospital? You must admit, no matter how involved you are, the patient owns at the very least 51 percent of the shares of this cancer investment.

We all need to put on our big girl panties and face cancer head on. Not one of us can curl up over in the corner and take this lying down if we are going to win. If that is the way you as a caregiver are going to play this game, then "You are the weakest link. Good Bye." You cannot make this about anyone else other than the patient because, while they are dry heaving, sweating, and crying, they will not be able to support you. That, is on you. Sorry to be so blunt, but honestly someone had to say it. We need to face it. This is difficult and bringing your "A" game is really the only option.

I have said throughout this book how important the caregivers are. I truly mean that. It is only true if they are being caregivers and not drama queens. I will have to admit though, having some drama that wasn't mine did entertain me many days of my recovery. When someone would call to check on *me* and then somehow make the conversation into a counseling session for *them*, I would have hours of drama to mull over that was better than anything on cable.

I would ask myself, *What is going on in their minds that makes them think like that? What struggles are they having and why? What is it like to be in their shoes?* I can sympathize with the fact that the world and all its craziness was still going on while I fought cancer. I really can. It's just that when a patient is fighting so hard, and is extremely tired; they just don't have the energy to tackle one more problem. They may not see that the dry cleaners losing your favorite shirt is a big deal, considering what they are going through. (#firstworldproblems as the kids say these days.) Most of the time I found the drama a distraction, and sometimes for a moment I didn't focus on me or what appointment was up next. Most of the time, I found them to be one big sociology experiment.

Over the years since cancer, I have found that no matter what I am struggling with, if I focus on others I start to feel better. This is a lesson for everyone. Yes, you are struggling, but by focusing on helping someone else you stop your pity party. As the caregiver, friend, or neighbor, you are stressed from your work, traffic, a phone call, your kids coach. Stop and ask yourself, what does your friend with cancer need? By removing yourself from your issues for a moment and trying to empathize with the person with cancer or their family you will be able to serve them and put life into perspective.

Now some advice for the patient, take a break and ask yourself, what is the normal world still doing? Was the commute bad on the way to work today? Did your friend's mom get out of the hospital? Yes, life seems daunting right now, remember when you talked to your friend about the coach and the new standards at work. Those issues are still there and causing stress for the outside world. Show that you are still the caring person you were before cancer. I will chat more on this subject a bit later. Stay tuned.

Please keep in mind:

*Matthew 5:7*
*Blessed are the merciful, for they will be shown mercy.*

Challenge yourself to find joy, and start by setting your priorities. Jesus. Others.Yourself.

## Chapter 18: And the Wiggie goes to…

One of the strongest pieces of advice I heard from this speaking panel of ladies at the convention came from Diem Brown. Her advice was to not take crap from *yourself!* Wow. My diagnosis taught me how to channel my orneriness and be an advocate for myself with medical professionals. I had even learned to show some orneriness with some caregivers that were a bit too pushy. The only thing I hadn't realized was I also needed to get ornery with myself. It was my own thoughts that were anchoring me down in doubt. I have always taken too much crap from my inner voice. The negative me is always louder than the positive me.

To this day, I am disappointed with how I handled my cancer. Yes. Read that again. I am actually upset I didn't handle cancer better. This won't surprise anyone who has seen my bullheadedness when I see a mountain I want to climb. I'm kinda competitive. If there was a trophy for the best cancer patient, I wanted it. I think the trophy should be a small bald figure, like the Oscars image, except the figure would be dressed in a hospital gown. One hand would be holding the back of the gown closed and the other would be holding the IV pole. We would call the award itself the *Wiggie*, but the ceremony would be *The Postiche Awards* because it sounds fancier. I would imagine we would make less of a hassle compared to other award shows and forgo the never ending red carpet and just have a rug, yes pun intended, at the door. Sure, it can be red. The ceremony wouldn't be drawn out over hours due to all nominees understanding how precious time is. Also no one would be asking, "Who are you wearing," because really what we are more interested in is, "What have you been eating?"

The ceremony would go something like this: For prettiest bald lady… Stacey Peterson. For the most energetic while hooked up to IV, the Wiggie goes to Stacey Peterson. The quickest to recover from yet another abdominal surgery, Stacey Peterson. For Rookie of the Year, MVP (most valuable patient), best supporting patient in a surgery, director of sound and lighting in a drama/comedy/action would all be mine, too. That's just how I roll.

Instead, what I saw was that I would not win any of those awards. I don't see myself winning these awards because there are many other people who were physically stronger, mentally focused, and emotionally wired in a more superior way. I walk away with the "honor of just being nominated."

When I look back at the roughly seven months I was in recovery, I personally see I should have done things differently. No one knows how they are going to respond when they are called up to the big leagues. I was not prepped for this journey and honestly the pitches were just coming too fast for me to really understand what was happening. I needed a pause and replay button, so I could slow things down instead of seeing things in real time. I sit back and think how I wish I could have walked into therapy with a smile on my face that lit up the room. Or that I would have had the energy to be a super mom to my baby, making sure I was caring for her with the right foods, swaddling techniques, and bonding time. I look at women who worked forty or more hours at their jobs, took care of their kids, and made sure there was supper on the table while they went through their treatment. The thing is, I struggle to do *that* to *my* standards even today when I am perfectly healthy.

There are amazing women in the world to show us that it can be done. It has been proven and on those days when we need a kick in the butt, we need these kinds of women to inspire us to at least take a shower and feed the pets. The truth of the matter is there isn't a right or wrong way to do cancer. I do realize on some level, I hold myself to a standard to which I don't hold anyone else. We all handle the treatments, surgery, and diagnosis differently, and sometimes we just need to tell the inner voice to *shut up*. Whether you are sick or healthy, the best way I have found to deal with the negative voice telling me I didn't do enough is by making a list.

No really. Lists are the answer to many of life's questions.

When I make a list of what I want to get done in a day I am more productive, and the truth is in the completed list, no matter what my inner voices are saying. I did get the laundry done, dishes washed, floors swept. I did call and make that appointment, I sent those emails, and purchased the birthday gift. At the end of the day when I have nothing else to do on my list for the day, my negative self doesn't have a leg to stand on because the proof is right there. *I DID GET SOMETHING DONE TODAY!* I was a success.

There, I didn't take crap from myself.

It's odd that in the times of our lives when we are bombarded with ugliness we aren't able to think of the next step. We have no clue how to start and we sit there in a state of befuddlement as if the directions for life are in a foreign language. You know the feeling, when you get those do-it-yourself assembly projects for furniture. We sit there reassuring ourselves that the college degree that is tucked safely away was actually signed. It's sheer hopelessness that seems to melt and mold onto our bodies and attach itself in some odd sci-fi way. During those times, it is tremendously hard to see what you are supposed to do next. My suggestion is to start off slowly and add the most common everyday task.

1. Make breakfast.
2. Shower.
3. Get dressed.

Okay, once those three things are done you feel better because you accomplished your list, but also because you are starting to feel human again. From there you will be able to tackle something small for your household…. I will load the dishwasher. Now, with less clutter your environment is uplifting. Next, look at the people around you… maybe write one of those thank-you notes or make your child's bed. Lastly, celebrate you: go for a walk outside or do your nails.

Miraculously, you went from not having direction to filling a good portion of your day. There is no doubt when you sit down at the end of the day you will feel you accomplished something. You will feel good and know tomorrow won't be too bad. You didn't allow yourself to tear *you* down.

Now, start making your own list of what you want to accomplish for today. Know you won't always get the check list done, but even doing part of it is a good way to motivate yourself to do more. Today you may not get the list done, but tomorrow might be the day you get the whole list done plus a few extras from yesterday.

I know this isn't a new idea. The research is out there, and the story goes that Charles Schwab over a hundred years ago, hired Ivy Ledbetter Lee to help his employers be more productive by making lists. His twist (and I completely I agree with him) is that after you have made your list, focus on the top six items and prioritize. Number them one to six. This simple but wonderful plan made Mr. Ivy a quick $25,000. I doubt when I suggest adding clipart and color-coding that I will be seeing any checks in the mail. No big deal. Just get yourself a list on old-fashioned paper, on your phone or even a white board, and start to get yourself moving in a powerful direction. (Cue the music to "We are the Champions" by Queen.") This allows you to stop hearing the negative voice and helps you to move closer to the Wiggie.

# Balance in Your Life

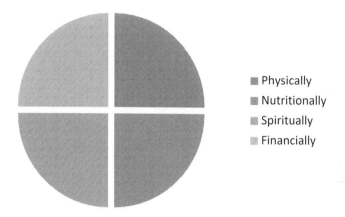

■ Physically
■ Nutritionally
■ Spiritually
■ Financially

Let's get Physical! I was a very active 28-year-old woman when I was diagnosed with stage one ovarian cancer. I'm not delusional; I know there are women in way better shape than I was at my time of diagnosis. There are women doing harder workouts while they are pregnant than I ever did as a college athlete or when I was training for any race. But I have to give myself some credit, I was always moving during my pregnancy and I think it made recovery easier.

It was this moving that got me ready for the race of a lifetime. The race to beat cancer was one I didn't sign up for and had no idea was even coming my way. I can officially say I did race and I did get the t-shirt. It started when I was just trying to be fit for my baby. In the long run, it got me in the shape I needed to be in to beat cancer. I was playing volleyball, softball and golf all while making sure I got in a long walk daily well into my sixth month of pregnancy. I was cutting back on the intensity of my playing as to not put the baby in harm's way, but I was moving and grooving with the best of them!

I recall in early June at about twenty-three weeks into pregnancy, I was still playing softball. (No judgment please). I had the basketball tummy showing. I imagine I looked like most pregnant women at twenty-three weeks, maybe a little more tummy considering I also had a tumor growing inside of me. I remember moving myself farther down in the batting order because I had the reality check that my chugging around the bases at this point was entertaining, but not the best for our team's record. There comes a time in everyone's life when they say, "Wow, that's what I look like?" In our heads we feel we are still preforming like Dorothy Hamill, Mary Lou Retton, Jennifer Finch, etc. The list goes on. For those of you who aren't old enough or sports minded, those are all elite Olympic athletes in their respective sports.

I am like everyone else. In our heads we see ourselves as an amazing athlete doing phenomenal things, but there comes a time when the world just sees us as performing something that needs to be on a gag real earning you $10,000.

I remember getting up to bat and nailing a solid bomb to left field. I took off and in my head I was graceful, elegant, and *oh so speedy*. The fact of the matter is I was running like I was pulling a plow behind me. I pulled into second base at the same time the ball was sailing in from the outfield, and I immediately called time out. I bent down to catch my breath. On any other day the hit would have gotten me an easy triple maybe even a homerun depending on the outfielder's arm. Needless to say, I was losing a step or two. I remember the catcher, a gal I had played against for a couple of years, came out of her crouched position, took a few steps toward me so she was in front of the home plate. She yelled out, "Are you pregnant?" As I was trying to catch my breath I laughed and nodded my head *yes*. In total disbelief she turned around and looked at the umpire, and they both smiled and shook their heads. "Well, okay. Game on."

Playing any of these sports during pregnancy didn't put my baby at danger. I played, but I played smart. It helped me stay physically and mentally healthy, and I think it explains why our child cannot stop moving. She was raised in an environment that never stopped moving.

I have always been the type of person that if you can distract me with a ball and get me to run around, I will be happy. However, if you tell me today we are going to work out, I will buck the system because I don't like to "work out." People will try to argue with me and tell me I do, but I say *nay nay*. I only like working out if I don't know I am working out. I once had a personal trainer friend who asked, "How could you have participated in sports your whole life, but say you don't like to work out?" Because training for a race or game, competing alongside my friends or playing rec ball was never a work out; it was just fun. You might be the same way. The important thing is for you to find something you like and move. Move every day. Move because you never know when it will be too hard to do so. Looking back, I can see this constant need to move and stay fit got me through three major abdominal surgeries in six months. My fitness level gave me continued energy on days when emotionally I was drained. I didn't know at the time that I was preparing myself for cancer and that is the point. You never know when there will be a challenge in your life. I encourage you to try and get the physical activity piece of the pie in your daily routine *now*.

I want to showcase to you what I have learned about the importance of fitness in my cancer treatment. I was doing something positive for myself, but it wasn't until much later that I realized how significant just a little bit of moving was for my health. You will see benefits when you include the smallest amount of fitness in your own treatment plan. No matter what your current health status is, we all know that adding even the smallest workouts will help you to reduce stress. There is no better time to reduce stress and give your body and mind a recess than when you are going through cancer treatment. Simple stretches or a short walk will allow your body to reboot and heal faster. The "runner's high" isn't only for major athletes in training. The rush of endorphins to our brains is real and can come with simply moving more. It's amazing that once you walk one trip down the hallway at the hospital, the second and third come quickly. You won't feel like doing it every day and that's okay. I strongly urge you to do an activity each day. It may not be walking; it may be simply stretching. Move. Get your body to feel alive.

In the lowest time of my recovery I was getting really down on myself, and I had a bad outlook on life. I would get up, walk downstairs and sit. Get up, go to the kitchen and sit. Followed by, me wandering into the living room for a nap. It was getting ugly. I had no energy to do anything. I had quickly gone from three nights of sports to doing nothing. Then finally I got the kick in the pants I needed. The simple suggestion *"Why don't you go for a walk?"* I started by taking a couple of simple trips up and down the stairs. At first, I was doing it out of spite and I wanted people to get off my back.

*Fine! Are you happy? I walked up and down the stairs; now give me back the remote.*

Soon my motivation turned to wanting to get away from people. I decided to take the long route to get the mail. This plan backfired on me though. Instead of having more time to myself where I could mope and be miserable, I started to feel better physically and mentally. I was more clear-headed, and I was happier. The fact was, the more energy I exerted to do this simple exercise, the more energy returned. I was getting that rush even from a simple walk.

We also know when we move and get exercise, we sleep better. For myself I notice an even greater outcome if I can exercise outside. There is something about being in the outdoors that refreshes me at that moment and then helps me to sleep in the evening. During the time of treatment, you may not be physically comfortable, and aches and pains may be keeping you from getting a good night's sleep. You may be extremely stressed, and getting a good night's sleep seems impossible. By adding a little bit of physical fitness to your daily routine, a good night's rest is more likely. Then of course, by getting a better night's rest you will feel better the following day. According to an online article in BioMed Central (www.biomedcentral.com/1471-2407/14/238), exercise has positive effects on the quality of life, physical function, muscular strength, and endurance, and can improve emotional well-being. Support from the University of Alberta in Edmonton, Canada stated that the outcome of recent studies shows physical activity not only acts as a deterrent for cancer, but can reduce cancer reoccurrences (www.ncbi.nlm.nih.gov/pmc/articles/PMC3507507/).

In a time when so much seems out of your control it is nice to see there is something you can do to help yourself and shift the numbers in your favor. I am sure, part of this study focused on the fact that general fitness raises our moods and improves cognitive functioning. When our minds are healthy and thinking more clearly, our bodies will follow suit.

I noticed that adding physical fitness to my days allowed me to spend time with people if I wanted, or extract myself from situations from which I needed a break. It is easier for some caregivers to step in and go for a walk with you rather than to sit and feel obligated to have a deep conversation about the elephant in the room. By getting out to the gym or on the walking trails the pressure to entertain is gone and both of you can just relax. At other times, it was nice to unplug from everyone and get the silence I needed. Going to a yoga class and not being interrupted by phone calls, texts, email, etc. is priceless. One other aspect to this freedom is by doing even minor workouts; you will regain strength, balance, and mobility, and allow yourself to have more freedom from some hovering caregivers. Bonus!

Let me add, it is very important to talk to your doctor before starting any exercise program to make sure you are physically healthy enough for the workouts of interest. Most doctors would recommend exercise three times a week as a critical part of cancer treatment. Many hospitals have fitness programs onsite or would be able to give you information about opportunities that are right for you. Please consider the strength of your immune system before heading to the gym or workout classes. Find something that helps you be active. Your goal should be for three times a week, but how you achieve that is completely up to you. There can be any combination. I think a variety of exercise is better, because after I get motivated to this process it doesn't take long for me to tire of doing the same thing over and over. Repetitiveness isn't great for your muscles or your mind either, growth comes from being challenged. Whenever I start out on a new routine, I always start with just walking. It won't take me long to get tired of walking, and I will want to add a little spice to my day. It was my goal in 2015 to try new things. At some point in my life, even though I know I will not be good at it, I want to try ZUMBA. Why? Just to say I did. I want to challenge myself to live just outside of my comfortable zone. If nothing else, I will be able to laugh hard at myself and work on my abs! This new attitude got me to try trampoline flips where I may or may not have given myself a concussion, as well as paddle boarding in Utah with the Southern Rockies as a back drop. Here is a list of some other things you may consider trying.

1. Yoga

2. Hiking
3. Tia Chi
4. Biking
5. Aqua Classes
6. Dance Classes
7. Snowshoeing
8. Skating, either on ice or on roller blades
9. Golf
10. Kayaking
11. Pilates

Then cool down with meditation, guided imagery, or prayer.

Start a routine this week and see how you do. Take a parking spot that will allow you to get more steps in or order water with your lunches. Start by making small changes, I promise you will see a difference. You will start to notice on the days you made those small tweaks in your behavior that you may have felt less stressed, slept better, or you reacted differently to treatment. At this point it is still early, but you can evaluate your schedule, see where you need improvements, and focus on what will make your pie fuller. Make it fun and challenge yourself. Push yourself to be just slightly uncomfortable. I've noticed it is easier and more fun to work out with someone by my side, even a pet. If schedules don't coincide, then find time to call, email, or text friends with your goals and updates, helpful hints, or encouragements. There are a few apps allowing workout buddies to track their team's success. It will start slowly, but you know who won the race between the tortoise and the hare, right?

I truly believe I was in a very healthy place, physically speaking, when I was diagnosed with cancer. That is why my abdominal surgeries didn't put me out of commission completely. I am not saying it couldn't have been better, but under the circumstances I think I was doing alright. Even today,

I certainly make mistakes on what I eat, drink, how much I weigh and how often I work out. The difference now is I am truly aware of it and do make decisions that will keep me around for as long as God wants me to be here. I could always do better and I will try; not all of us can be on the cover of a fitness magazine. We should look for progression, not perfection. If you are monitoring how many steps you are walking per day, ask yourself "Are you increasing each day?" If you are looking at reducing sugar or calories from drinks is your water intake increasing? Monitor your sleep; are you sleeping better and waking feeling rested? Keep these notes and prove to yourself that you are making a difference. Athletes do the same thing when they are training. Is my time faster than last week? Am I lifting more than I was before? How have my averages changed? For my healthy readers you, too, should be thinking about a fitness program. What will you do to make physical activity a part of your weekly routine now? Be physically prepared for a fight you hope you never have to fight.

The next piece of this graph is being healthy spiritually. My advice to you is to get in the best shape you can because you never know what tomorrow brings. No one knows how they will react when they get called up to play in the cancer game. If you are not currently supported by a faith community, I challenge you today to research what churches are closest to you. When are their services? Consider joining. We all want to think we would be in the running for a Wiggie if the cancer call came tomorrow, but we just don't know. I suggest forming a strong foundation with God and your church community while you are healthy and life is easier. You will need these tools sharpened and well-oiled at the time of any fight. Diagnosis or tragedy is not the time to use them for the first time. God is waiting for you. He wants you to talk to Him. If the relationship is not as strong as you'd like it to be, work on it. Spend five minutes with Him today; it will lead you into a relationship like no other. Trust me you won't be disappointed.

Think of it this way: your community has a hardware store, right? It is full of tools, manuals, and some employees that could help you make some amazing improvements in your home. First you would purchase the right tools, then obtain a specific manual and probably ask a couple of questions of the associates to make your home improvement complete. Your local church is the same way. It has the tools, the manual (Bible), and the teachers you need to build *your* personal improvement plan. Reach out to them and load up your spiritual tool box now.

Many times, it takes you getting blindsided before you really know what you are made of. Just like getting yourself into good physical shape so, heaven forbid, if you go into surgery tomorrow you could recover quickly. I feel you need to work out spiritually as well. I will not tell you what you should do exactly to achieve this because it will be different for everyone. I simply suggest you find fellowship with friends, try to understand your earthly role, and find a church that will strengthen your relationship with your Creator. I say all this because many people just want to reach out and have a spiritual life after there is a crisis. I say, have an "insurance policy" before you feel desperate and alone.

The foundation of my faith was something I had been working on since I was a small child. I prayed often and went to church weekly. I thought I was strong in my faith, but I had never realized for the iron of our faith to be strong it must be tested in fire. I was blessed and never had been tested. My faith still had weak points that were filled with doubt, fear, and at times lack of faith in God and myself. I won't beat myself up over this fact because I know this is normal, and it is at the lowest times in our lives that evil attacks those weak points and raises doubt. This is what the devil does best. When the serpent rears its head in Genesis 3, it plays games with Eve, asking her tricky questions to raise doubt and then lying to her. The devil is working on all of us today, too. He is raising doubt in our minds and shoving lies in our face. We need to go places where the truth and God's love is given to us. Through prayer, song, and fellowship we will find strength to turn away from the enemy and stay strong. We will have the answers we need and be able to say, *"Get behind me Satan." Matthew 16:23*

We must remember not to listen to doubt, but to equip ourselves with God's words. We are told in 2 Timothy 1:7, *"for God gave us a spirit not of fear but of power and love and self-control."* I remind myself of this often. God doesn't want us to be scared. I hear myself referring to this verse often when I see our daughter is fearful. God is our Father. He loves us and to see any of His children living in fear crushes Him, just like it does with earthly parents. God is going to do everything He can for us, just like a parent makes sure that there is a night light in the corner and that the doors are locked.

*Romans 8:31*
*"If God is for us, who can be against us?"*

The subject of having God as our teammate comes up a lot in conversation in a house that is as sports minded as ours. *Imagine, if God were literally standing on the pitcher's mound; who would beat you?* So, put God on your team. Let Him guide you and call all the pitches. You will win, I promise.

My two favorite verses are Jeremiah 29:11 as I shared earlier and the verse Matthew 10:29-31 *"Can you not buy two sparrows for a penny? And yet not one falls to the ground without your Father knowing. Why, every hair on your head has been counted. So, there is no need to be afraid; you are worth more than many sparrows."* To this day hearing this scripture is like a mic drop. Bam! *The defense rests, Your Honor.* And *Ta da!* all wrapped together! Enough said! You can't argue with it.

While I was writing this book, I talked to caregivers about their journey through cancer, and the common thread they shared was they relied on their spiritual strength. It was something they had been working on their whole lives. The best thing I can say is it's nice to already have the parachute strapped on when the door of the plane opens. Start forming this relationship with God and fill as many holes in your faith as you can before your crisis comes. There will be a crisis. It may not be cancer, but there will be something. Will you be ready?

Again, hospitals usually have the local information you need for spiritual support. There are oncology chaplains for one-on-one counseling, sacred spaces for reflection such as a meditation room or chapel, as well as patient navigators who will be able to guide you and your caregivers to the services you need. If you are already working on your spiritual health before you are diagnosed, it will be easy to make the call to the prayer warriors in your own church or to your parent group or women's group for support to openly pray and ask for prayers. It's one of those things you may not think a lot about when you are healthy, but it sure does consume your mind when you are sick.

One last bit I want to cover when it comes to your spiritual strength concerns prayer. It was during this health scare when I found myself being too exhausted, too emotional, and too scatterbrained to even form prayers. I would sit down and want to launch into a long dialogue of my feelings and fears. Instead I would sit down and get ready to pray, but then become completely lost. *"How do I start?"*

Many times, I would just feel lost and want to say, *"You know what I need. Amen."* It was just hard to put the words together. I guess chemo brain, being extremely tired, and feeling substantial amounts of stress had finally made me speechless. I had never experienced being too wiped out to form the words to a prayer before. It shocked me. I strongly encourage you to form the relationship with God now and to create your prayer warrior phone chain so that when you are at a loss a simple phone call will get the ball rolling. This is comparable to Exodus 17:12, when Moses' arms grew tired and he was not able to finish God's will alone. He had Aaron and Hur hold them up. We all need this at different times in our lives. Once we have these people beside us, we use their words to help us travel the road God wants us to take. When we are too wiped out to form a prayer, it is important to reach out to others, and they can hold you up with their prayers.

Memorized prayers, which I use often in my Catholic faith, were my way of taking the first step into my Father's peaceful embrace. Not everyone is familiar with prewritten or memorized prayers, and instead they tend to speak freely to God. I do practice spontaneous prayers as well. However, there are times when the words just won't come, and at those moments it is comforting to rely on the words of others to express my mixed emotions. There have been many nights when I wrestled with the sheets, and found a calm mind by reciting the Memorare:

> *Remember, O most gracious Virgin Mary,*
> *that never was it known that anyone who fled to thy*
> *protection, implored thy help or sought thy intercession,*
> *was left unaided. Inspired by this confidence,*
> *I fly unto thee, O Virgin of virgins my Mother;*
> *to thee do I come, before thee I stand, sinful and*
> *sorrowful; O Mother of the Word Incarnate,*
> *despise not my petitions, but in thy mercy, hear and*
> *answer me. Amen.*

Knowing that Mary is listening and will intercede for me gives me the confidence to breathe. Mary is going to protect me. Mary is going to be like any good mother and listen to me. She will console me, and though I am a sinner I find solace in these memorized words.

I can also remember the peace prayer of St. Francis from the melodic tune I grew up with and sang in choir.

*Lord, make me an instrument of your peace:*
*where there is hatred, let me sow love;*
*where there is injury, pardon;*
*where there is doubt, faith;*
*where there is despair, hope;*
*where there is darkness, light;*
*where there is sadness, joy.*

*O divine Master, grant that I may not so much seek*
*to be consoled as to console,*
*to be understood as to understand,*
*to be loved as to love.*
*For it is in giving that we receive,*
*it is in pardoning that we are pardoned,*
*and it is in dying that we are born to eternal life.*
*Amen.*

I have been reminded many times to serve others through these familiar words and am humbly reminded I should seek to console rather than want consoling.

The church tradition was for educated men to lead prayer, and the repetition of prayers was a way for the uneducated congregation to be a part of any service and to learn about God in general. This is a fact in all of church history and can still be seen in general education today when we try to teach children. Nursery rhymes, poems, songs, and prayers are all memorized, broken down and shared so children will be able to learn the information. Furthermore, in 1st Corinthians verse 12, the gifts of the Holy Spirit are explained. As humans, we all have different kinds of gifts, and if my gift is not words, then I am going to use the words of others to guide me to a closer relationship with God. At times when I cannot find the words, I will rely on the gifts of those who came before me, and I find peace.

God Himself gave us Matthew 6:9, *The Our Father*, and Luke 1:28, *The Hail Mary*. The psalms are another example because they were written as poems, but were recited as prayers and even sung. This repetitive type of prayer you find in song is such a blessing because you find yourself praying and humming along to the tune later, essentially praying over and over again. *"When you sing, you pray twice."* This is a misquote from St. Augustine, but the idea is we create a file in our brains with these sung words. Sometimes the Holy Spirit guides those words and the tune back to us and we start to pray/sing again. This doesn't typically happen with simple words we hear.

Memorized prayers are not rants, simply maps to bring us closer to the Father, Jesus, and the Holy Spirit through the art of speech. When these memorized prayers are said with an open heart of love they can open the door to hearing what our Lord wants us to hear. If you are talking with God with an open heart and using my words, your words, or a memorized prayer from long ago, God is listening. He isn't going to worry as much as we do about the author.

Communication with God means you need to sit sometimes, be still, and not say anything. John 10:27 says, *"My sheep hear My voice, and I know them, and they follow Me."* Hear His voice. Truly hear it and wash it around in your mind and heart. Let your soul marinate. Listening, instead of worrying about what to say, is the key. Just remember: we have one mouth and two ears for a reason. Many times, we can learn a lot more from listening than always being the one talking.

Let's look at nutrition. This is something we naturally should be working on when we are healthy to be at our own personal best. We need to be avoiding the fatty, sugar-loaded, yummy goodness that makes life extremely enjoyable. We all know it, but very few of us actually do it. This behavior, of eating processed foods, of course can lead to health problems, but it can also lead us to having a slower recovery after surgeries and our bodies not responding as positively to cancer treatments and medications. A nutritionist can help you easily add the right foods back into your diet when your appetite returns. Nutritional therapy is another way for you to fight back against cancer. I believe that many cancers are based from the amounts of sugars we eat, the chemicals on our foods and our diet choices. Talking with a nutritionist can help you find foods that will help boost your immune system, speed recovery after surgery, limit digestive issues so that you can prevent malnutrition and avoid side effects of treatment. The website for the American Cancer Society has a *list!* It contains tabs such as recipes, managing weight gain, diets for before treatment begins, diets for when you have mouth sores, and more. There are also some great companies catering directly to cancer patients. They are able to create options for you, and have meals delivered directly to your home for easy preparation. This will refuel your body the right way. Many hospitals have nutritional resources and can assist you in finding healthy food demonstrations or in finding companies that will assist you in making healthier choices.

1. www.dana-farber.org/nutrition
2. www.magnoliamealsathome.com/
3. www.momsmeals.com/about-us/
4. www.savorhealth.com/about-us/why-savor-health/

*These companies are in alphabetical order and I do not have any personal experience using them. If you have someone who keeps asking how they can help, ask him or her to research these companies to see if the company will deliver in your area, or to call your local hospital to see if they will be holding any classes. Hospitals may also have a dietician who could help specifically with a cancer patient's diet and give you recipes or other sites that may be helpful.

I always felt very lucky that my oncologist never restricted my diet. He never suggested I change my diet. His comment was to eat whatever you want that will not make you feel nauseated. That kind of rule I could handle. There was a time towards the end of my treatment when I felt lousy, and if someone would have told me I needed to eat "this" or not eat "that," I think I would have slapped them. I suggest starting off slowly and adding one thing at a time that will put you just on the outside of completely comfortable. Maybe you will start juicing, taking vitamins, or maybe just stop having bacon for every meal. Challenge your comfort and try something new. Your doctor can be a great asset in helping you make a well-rounded pie chart.

One last thing to round out our pie: financial health. This bit of advice is most important for those readers who are healthy and have time to start making changes today. The financial gurus tell us to squirrel away at least six months of wages in case some tragedy happens. This can most easily be done by setting aside assets in
1. A simple savings account.
2. A money market account.
3. An online brokerage account.

The key here is to make sure the funds are easily accessible and invested conservatively.

If you are going to make changes to our finances, then you need to adjust all parts of our life. Make changes to your physical health, nutrition and spiritual health, just as you do with your finances. You are worth the investment.

I want you to think about this: if you were told tomorrow you had cancer would you be physically, spiritually, nutritionally, and financially as healthy as you could be?

## Chapter 20: Great Bible verses to guide you.

**Matthew 11:28** *"Come to me, all you who are weary and burdened, and I will give you rest."* This is listed first because I cannot read it without also singing it. It sticks with you and comes back to remind you that God wants you to be at peace. Rest, and He will comfort you like a parent with a child.

**Jeremiah 17:14** *"Heal me, O LORD, and I will be healed; save me and I will be saved, for you are the one I praise."*

**Mark 5:34** He said to her, *"Daughter, your faith has healed you. Go in peace and be freed from your suffering."* God is all powerful and can heal all. He desperately wants you to trust in Him and to reach out to Him. After suffering for twelve years a woman knew in her heart that Jesus could heal her if she only touched his cloak. This undying faith moves her to Jesus, and essentially healing. I pray the same for you.

**Isaiah 41:10** *"So do not fear, for I am with you; do not be dismayed, for I am your God. I will strengthen You and help you; I will uphold you with my righteous right hand."*

**Ecclesiastes 3:1-3** *"For everything there is a season, and a time for every matter under heaven: a time to be born, and a time to die; a time to plant, and a time to pluck up what is planted; a time to kill, and a time to heal; a time to break down, and a time to build up."* Sound familiar? Some of our favorite songs are inspired by scripture. This is a season of your life, not the whole forecast.

**Psalm 30:2** *"Lord my God, I called to you for help, and you healed me."* Why not put this to long term memory and repeat it to yourself?

**John 16:20** *"In all truth I tell you, you will be weeping and wailing while the world will rejoice; you will be sorrowful, but your sorrow will turn to joy."*

**Philippians 4:6-7** *"Be anxious for nothing, but in everything by prayer and supplication with thanksgiving let your requests be made known to God. And the peace of God, which surpasses all comprehension, will guard your hearts and your minds in Christ Jesus."*

**2 Timothy 1:7** *"For God has not given us a spirit of fear, but of virtue, and of love and of self-restraint."* We are not supposed to be afraid. We are supposed to trust, to rely on God. Satan wants us to be scared. He wants us to doubt. Do not let him win.

# Chapter 21: Taking more time to realize what's around you.

I stated earlier in this book a few things that bring me joy. They were in no particular order and were just a few of the things rolling around in my head as I prepared to write this book. Since that time and through this beautiful journey I have only come up with more. It is amazing how many things you can appreciate when you take the time. As adults we need to make a conscious effort but as toddlers we just soaked these things up. 1 Corinthians 13:11 "When I was a child, I used to talk like a child, and see things as a child does, and think like a child; but now that I have become an adult, I have finished with all childish ways." I challenge you to keep some childish ways. It is very easy to be consumed with work, bills, health, cleaning, and all the other grown-up-non-fun stuff. The challenge is to roll the windows down and sing at the top of your lungs, badly and maybe not even the right lyrics. Why? *Because you can!*

*Matthew 18:3*
*"Truly I tell you, unless you change and become like little children, you will never enter the kingdom of heaven.*

Realizing what is around us, and more importantly that it is all given to us to share, love, and respect is an amazing gift. As a toddler, we enjoy exploring every little aspect of life. We feel the uncontrollable urge to put our fingers, no our arms all the way up to our scuffed elbows, into that sticky mixture of life; playing and digging just so we can wipe it on things. We can't help but run wildly with abandon through open fields (or crowded stores, for that matter). Our little bodies and spirits can't be wrangled. If you have ever been to a young child's soccer game it will take five minutes before a coach or parent utters the phrase, "It's like herding cats out there." Somewhere between us learning to walk and us getting more involved in society, we lose the freedom to unfocus. We are broken down to conform, and keep moving to achieve a goal. The goal of just being in the moment is gone. The circle of life is complete when you see the elderly laughing and acting carefree. I utterly enjoy the greeting cards where the old people are in their scarves, helmets, and goggles and laughing in a sidecar of a motorcycle. Why wait until we are older to enjoy life again? *see image at the end of the chapter

Continuing the "simple things" list from chapter eleven...
51. Listening and watching a large flock of Canadian geese fly overhead.
52. The smell of fresh baked bread.
53. Sunbeams.
54. Snow, before anyone walks on it.
55. When someone pays for your lunch.
56. The security you can give a baby animal in your warm arms, and watch as the animals relinquishes all its' fears.
57. A really good laugh.
58. Wind chimes.
59. Absolute quiet.
60. Rain storms.
61. Cream cheese frosting.
62. Sleeping with the windows open.
63. Receiving snail mail.
64. The smell of a charcoal grill.
65. The excitement of planning a trip.
66. Old people holding hands.
67. Technology that works.
68. A door being held open.
69. A smile.
70. No lines at a store, drive-thru, or event.
71. Long weekends.
72. Blue pens (I can't stand writing in black).
73. Appointments that actually start on time.
74. Movie popcorn.
75. The smell of bed sheets dried outside.

76. The beach.
78. The oldies music stations.
79. Reminiscing with reruns of shows you grew up watching.
80. The atmosphere in any professional sporting event.
81. The clearance aisle.
82. Homemade quilts.
83. First flowers of spring.
84. The fall colors adorning the trees.
85. A "properly" made Bloody Mary. The worst one I ever had included horseradish.
86. A cold red beer. (If you are from the Midwest you know what I am talking about…cheers!)
87. Family photos.
88. Antique stores.
89. No traffic.
90. Photography, art, decorating, cooking, etc. classes.
91. Deviled eggs.
92. Sitting in a fairly empty church.
93. Stargazing.
94. Fireworks.
95. Knowing how to play an instrument.
96. Sharing your gift with others.
97. Being able to lose those 5 pounds.
98. Magazines that don't have the postcard advertisements in them.
99. A new outfit.
100. Notes from your kids.
101. Dogs hanging out car windows.
102. Old country songs.
103. Watching a child taste a lime for the first time.

Sodahead.com
We need to change now and be like children and enjoy the life around us.

## Chapter 22: "Yes officer, *that* is my circus and *those* are *my* monkeys."

Many times, throughout the months I fought cancer I would be distracted by the caregivers in my life: the family and friends that were in my inner most circle. These people became my circus performers. I would see cancer impacting all of us in different ways. As the patient, I had the physical scars, the draining schedule and in my opinion, the heaviest baggage. However, there were many people who responded to my cancer in a way that kept my head on a swivel from one circus act to another. I don't feel that my troop of monkeys was any different from your close-knit circle. Sure, there are little differences in the performers, but basically all circus acts are the same.

To this day when I deal with my performers it feels like I'm in a true balancing act. My circus is made up of the usual acts; the monkeys, fire eaters, the tight rope walkers, and clowns. To balance all these performers and their unique skills, one must understand different languages and appreciate all their talents. Communication is key when working with any group and our family circus is no different. Sadly, communicating effectively with each other isn't our strongest skill. That is not to say we don't *talk* to each other. On the contrary, the problem is we *do* talk to each other. At the end of any family gathering, not just during medical emergencies, it is a given that something will be said and someone will be offended by what they heard, by the tone used, or the body language that it is wrapped in. This creates a circus for every holiday, family reunion, and heck, even funerals. Your family may be the same.

*"The single biggest problem in communication is the illusion that it has taken place."*
*~George Bernard Shaw*

There have been many family occasions as I travel back down the long road that takes me home, when I ask myself, "Did that just happen?" Let me give you an example. The words used were, "Why did you get me this?" but after years of training I am able to translate that and hear, "This is not what I was expecting. Thank you!"

Here's another example. "Jesus Christ, what the hell were you thinking?" is what is said at the supper table, but I chose to hear "I am glad you are alright!" This skill takes a while to perfect and it isn't taught in any school, but the sooner I learned to perfect it the better off I was emotionally to deal with the wild creatures at my circus.

Last example, "Oh, good God!" translates into "You may want to rethink your answer."

Being a linguist with a snarky sense of humor proved to be beneficial as I watched people deal with my cancer diagnosis. The years of translating what was said into what was meant helped as I eased into a comfy chair to watch everyone else try to figure out the cancer thing. Managing cancer from my vantage point wasn't making it clearer. So trying to decipher cancer through other people's interpretations was worth a try. I watched as people said stupid things, responded in inhumane ways and clearly fumbled along. I would than try and hear what they meant, imagine what actions were intended and be sympathetic to the struggle we all felt.

I never really wanted to focus on me while I traveled through cancer town anyway, and thank goodness there was enough entertainment going on around me that I didn't have to. My circus was never boring. My performers were acting and saying things that made for great reality TV.

One of the most used phrases around my house these days came from my cancer journey. It's simple, to the point, a little cold, but honest. It's just four small words. "It's not about you." Now, I never used this phrase during my cancer treatments, but later when I sat back and started thinking about what had happened I realized it would have come in handy. For instance, when other people would come up to me and ask how I was, and suddenly they would get all choked up and too weepy to visit. They would need a hug, and I would just stop trying to answer the original question and make sure they had enough tissues.

Or when someone wanted to tell me about their brother's coach's nephew's friend who once had a scare of possible cancer and how they knew exactly what I must be feeling. I would bite my tongue, smile politely and listen. (I would strongly advise you don't tell a cancer patient you understand how they are feeling. Even if you have been in a similar situation it is better to remain silent and listen. You will be able to learn a lot.) Looking back I wish I would have said, "This isn't about you."

How about when friends struggled seeing my activity level decrease so I sat alone and didn't get in their way of a normal routine and activities. "This isn't about you!" Remember, your challenge as a friend is to be creative and figure out how you can meet patients halfway. My job as the patient was to deal with cancer. I think you have the way better deal.

There were people who would start crying because they were scared, or they would start destroying their own life because of the stress of my cancer. I should have shouted *"THIS ISNT ABOUT YOU!"*

So, when I look back on the ugliness I remember the non-medical parts of cancer that hurt so much. I can only imagine the difficulty of being a friend who watches the patient endure the cancer trip, and I want to say to you a quote by Albert Camus: *"Don't walk behind me; I may not lead. Don't walk in front of me; I may not follow. Just walk beside me and be my friend."* The true job of the circus performers is to make sure the show goes on and that there is enough cotton candy.

My tangle with cancer led the people closest to me, my performers, to cope in many different ways. They each would fall into different roles throughout cancer and the ride would just continue around and around, carousel music and all. I noticed that sometimes the easiest way to cope was to go into **juggler mode**. This required no time for feelings, just tasks. That way people were "helping" get the black and white handled. My life was being juggled and tasks were taken care of by some of my closest team members. The only problem is, there was a lot of gray. I found myself asking many days "Who is going to take care of the gray?"

Then there were the people who wanted to live in the **house of mirrors**. It was as if they were standing in front of the exaggerated mirrors and they were starting to become the images. Picture these people standing in front of the "cancer mirror." They would see themselves heavy with the weight of the diagnosis, tired from the treatment, and consumed with the feeling that this hand of fate was not fair for *them*. I do understand that it must have been hard to be in the audience watching the cancer show. But as a true audience member you don't know for sure what it's like to be in the circus, to have cancer and not just take on the image of being scared, stressed, and lonely. I had people coming to my circus telling me that the cancer circus job was hard, the hours were long, cleaning up after the elephants was grueling and the pay wasn't paying the bills. Really? I know I own the circus.

This was hard to hear because I was tired myself. I really didn't have the energy to be there for them; I was having a hard-enough time just having enough energy to get through my own day. The cancer circus *is* hard. We all need to find strength deep within ourselves and make sure we aren't dumping on others. If we can manage to carry our own share it becomes a lot easier. This fight is truly about all of us.

The **clowns** created their own distraction from reality. Their mind set seemed to say, "Look at me." Clowns are good at creating diversions so that the other parts of the big top can be set up. The clowns in my circus were definitely fumbling over themselves, spraying themselves with seltzer, and sitting on whoopee cushions all while time ticked away. I recall back to watching the circus as a kid and thinking that the clowns were causing delays in the real show. That they were creating messes to clean up and headaches for the ring master. The clowns in my actual cancer circus weren't much different.

Lastly, I want to look at the **entertainers** who just wanted to be shot out of the cannon. They conveniently were not available for comment. You'd turn away for a second, turn back and suddenly they were flying 50 feet over your head into a net 100 yards away on the other end of the tent. That's them, just waving from a safe distance away. This was popular in my circus and really became a big part of the show. I can understand team members were busy but this cancer thing is hard. I'd suggest figuring out what it is you can do to contribute. Find a way only you can help and get back into the show and help the patient. Be the one who holds the rope for the acrobats or trains the bear.

The struggle and chaos of the circus was real for everyone. We all did what we were capable of doing at the time. Now I can accept and find some humor in everyone's reactions. I strongly suggest to patients to try and see the humor and take what people can offer: capes, red noses, leotards and all.

The important thing to understand is everyone has a strength, and if everyone did something they were comfortable with, then the black, white, gray and every color in between would be handled. To win against cancer we must have a variety of people on our team. The circus will run smoothly and be orchestrated very well if you can learn to create a balanced group.

The true ring master of my circus was of course God. He was balancing all of the people in my life and brought the right surgical staff to me when I needed them. I can thank my husband for the support and continuous love. I can thank my new baby for loving me, accepting me and giving me something to get excited about. I can thank my mom, dad, sisters and brothers, who helped clean my house, became welcomed visitors, volunteered to babysit, and brought comfort items. I can thank friends who called, wrote letters, brought food, cleaned toilets, and went out of their way to help with our weekly tasks.

Remember, there is a spot for everyone in the cancer circus. If you are in the wings of the show you have the advantage of being able to see things differently than the main performers. Your challenge as one of the spectators is to see how you can make a difference and contribute to the show. Now, if you are the patient remember, this is a variety show. Let everyone play their part and take some time to watch your monkeys do their thing.

*1 Peter 4:10*
*Each one of you has received a special grace, so, like good stewards responsible for all these varied graces of God, put it at the service of others.*

# Chapter 23: What I think you need to hear today.

**1. You can do anything with God's help.**
There will be moments, some moments that don't seem to end, when you feel powerless. That may be true if you were alone, but you are not alone. God our Savior is with you, and He will carry you through this moment with His love and strength.

**2. You are beautiful.**
Your beauty as a person is rooted deep in your soul. It was started before you were ever born. It has grown from that point and shines outwardly reaching all of us. Your beautiful essence has touched so many. Your smile. Your touch. Your presence.

**3. You are stronger than you think.**
No one knows what they are truly capable of until they have been tested. This moment is testing you. It has pushed you so far away from comfortable that you aren't even sure you know how comfortable feels. You made it through yesterday and the day before. Today I want you to think of one thing you are going to do. "I am going to sit up." If it takes you all day, accomplish that one thing, then so be it. You *can* do it and *will* do it. One thing at a time. I was five when my grandmother died and the only song I remember from her funeral is "One Day at Time," by Kris Kristofferson and Marijohn Wilkins.

> *One day at a time sweet Jesus. That's all I'm asking from you. Just give me the strength, To do every day what I have to do. Yesterday's gone sweet Jesus. And tomorrow may never be mine. Lord help me today, show me the way. One day at a time.*

4. **God has this: just let Him heal you.**
   Can you trust that? Can you say someone has gotten you here, through that one time and the other? Can you say there is someone in charge, more powerful than you? You are here for a reason and if, for some reason God is not here to physically heal you, then let Him spiritually heal you. Gain acceptance of God in your heart (He has already accepted you) and let God love on you. Let Him bring you inner peace and an abundance of love.

5. **Breathe**.
   Slow your mind. Try and understand that you need to stop and to breathe.

6. **Do something you enjoy.**
   Do this today, or for at least a solid moment. Find your joy. I'm sure it has been awhile since you could fold those words around in your mind and create the picture of concrete, ear-to-ear, chest warming, peace-creating joy. Recently when I was asked to visualize *joy* I had no idea what that would look like. Joy? Happiness, okay I can see that. Joy, I had no idea. What is that you enjoy, what brings you real joy? Discover it. Live it. While soaking up the sun, taking a hot shower, sitting in church, or walking in nature, slow your mind down enough to identify your joy.

7. **Give a hug and RECEIVE A HUG.**
   I know that I set up barriers to protect my mental state. I answer questions like "How are you?" with a robotic reflex of "Fine, and you?" I slap on a smile and nod and wave when I need to share the tears or frustration I am sometimes feeling. During those times when we are simply going through the motions in some mechanical way, we need to stop. We need to make ourselves, and our responses to life around us, human again. Don't just

lean in for the conventional reception of squeeze, pat, pat. Accept the hug and let it ooze into your cells.

## 8. I know this isn't any fun.

Yes, I do think you need to hear that. Please know that I empathize with you. This current hand you've been dealt doesn't look so great. Remember it's all what you do with it, though. Don't automatically fold. Play the cards out, put on your poker face. We have all seen a game of cards, or professional sports match take a sudden change. I think soccer is the worst. You have been glued to the TV for 85 minutes. You get up because you just know that it will go into extra time. Just as you get to the cupboard you hear "GOOOAAALLLL!" Right now, it feels like you are in the 85$^{th}$ minute of the longest game of your life! Hold on, because the moment of celebration with your team is about to happen.

## 9. You aren't alone.

You do have a team with you: a medical team, a social team, a prayer team. Today, from whom do you feel you need support from? Send that text, make that phone call, or visit your church. Be courageous and make a small step in the direction you need today.

## 10. You are doing this journey perfectly.

I needed to hear this one. I had it in my mind that I was supposed to be looking a particular way, eating a certain way, working a set amount. However, you are dealing with this mess is fine. Tomorrow you can make changes if you want, but honestly, if you are alive then you have the opportunity to step into your big girl panties and break down some doors! Even a small door will work.

## Chapter 24: Lesson #101 Paying it forward

Now we must talk about giving back. Depending on where you are in this whole process, this may seem impossible. The fact of the matter is, you can give back in several ways.
1. While you are at the hospital for treatment, maybe there are other patients you can sit with who don't have family to support them.
2. Write encouraging notes for patients, caregivers, or staff.
3. You can contact the American Cancer Society or a local cancer chapter and ask to do volunteer work like knitting caps for patients.

Figure out how much time you can give back and what talents you can share. If you are feeling well enough, the American Cancer Society has a program where volunteers drive patients to their treatments.

Two years after I was diagnosed I helped with this exact volunteer opportunity. I was happy to provide this service because I realized how fortunate I had been to have friends and family take me to appointments. If you lived by yourself, didn't have family around, or didn't yourself drive, getting to treatments would be a challenge. This is not a time when you need one more challenge. There was one old man who was always angry – *the* walking, breathing definition of a curmudgeon. I did feel for the man. Having this reoccurrence of cancer was hitting him hard. It wasn't always fun to bring him to appointments, but I needed to remember this was not about me. Taking him to his appointments was always something I felt good about doing once it was over. I plastered a smile on my face, which I think just made him saltier, and I would make light conversation. He was the male version of the Saturday Night Live character Debbie Downer played by Rachel Dratch. I don't hold that against him, and I am choosing to believe that even though I was healthy and happy and bouncing in like Little

Miss Sunshine, he didn't secretly hate me. I want to believe, though he never would say it, that he appreciated the time and conversation I provided for him. I know for me, at least, giving back in this way was an amazing opportunity. This opportunity gave me insight and a higher appreciation for the people who had been on my team. A maturing occurred inside of me, an understanding unknown to a survivor, but familiar to a caregiver.

If you are feeling healthy enough, I suggest finding a local chapter for a particular cause in your area. When I moved to Dallas, TX in 2010, I did just that. I had been volunteering with local races, fundraising, and the American Cancer Society for nine years. When I moved though, I was determined to do more for ovarian cancer specifically. I was thrilled to find out I could split my time volunteering for a national office and a local chapter. I was lucky to only have to drive thirty minutes from my home and some days I could volunteer by sending out emails from my home. I was able to make my own schedule and give as little or as much of my time as my schedule would allow. In these types of offices there are many opportunities for a volunteer. I have been able to help with race day committees, advertising, promotions, mailings, preparing patient comfort totes, speaking to small groups, preparing race day packets, working at health fairs, planning survivor events, and much more. Patients need the organization, and the organization needs you! The success of the non-profit sector is dependent on volunteers and anything you do is never too small.

Something else you may want to think over is whether you will be willing to be involved in clinical trials. Most people do not know enough about them and trials should not be ruled out. I didn't hear about them until I was five years from diagnosis and because of my diagnosis I didn't qualify.

According to the Octane website, clinical trials are a significant reason why the survival rates of childhood cancers have increased from lower than fifty percent five years after diagnosis to over eighty percent. Many women with ovarian cancer are not aware of clinical trials and therefore cannot give back and help change the outcome for ovarian cancer victims. Eighty percent of children diagnosed will see their five-year cancer-free anniversary, where less than thirty percent of ovarian cancer patients will be able to celebrate this same accomplishment. Please ask your doctor if there are any trials you qualify for and how to get started. When you are a part of a clinical trial you are getting the newest treatment options. This may mean you will have better survival than patients who are using what was been used for decades with substandard results. Also, the results of clinical trials demonstrate that patients monitored during trials will do better than patients receiving similar care outside of a trial.

For you, I recommend being open to your treatment plan and asking your physician if clinical trials will be a part it. Stop, and hear all the options and possibilities so you can make an informed decision.

Without judging and pointing my finger, I want to say if you have been given the lemon of cancer, then make lemonade out of it. Make lemonade for a lot of people in fact. Being a part of a clinical trial is being a part of a solution. Men and women from all cancer groups can be a part of clinical trials and in doing so they end up providing answers for the medical community on what treatments are working and they help get us all closer to finding answers. If you don't decide to do a trial to help the future patients, then what hope do we have that this will ever end?

If you don't qualify for clinical trials or if the previous ideas don't fit into your comfort zone, then you can always make a monetary donation to a local chapter for your cancer. Non-profit organizations rely on grants, fundraisers, and donations to keep education and research progressing. If you are blessed in a way that allows you to give back with a monetary gift, I suggest doing your research and figuring out how your money will be used. Be diligent and find out which non-profit supports your passion. Do you want the focus to be on research or education? Do you want the donation to fund a program that helps patients specifically or promotes public awareness? Ask questions and see if there is a particular segment of the organization where your donation can make an impact. Get creative and find a way to give back.

Survivors, you are still here. Do what you can to bring a blessing to someone else. Acts 20:35 says, *"By every means I have shown you that we must exert ourselves in this way to support the weak, remembering the words of the Lord Jesus, who himself said, 'There is more happiness in giving than in receiving.'"*

We've talked about giving of your time, your talents, physically helping through science research, and monetary giving. These are all important. Any one or combination will be appreciated and potentially save lives. I know cancer happens to all of us for a reason. We don't always see that. We don't always understand it but the cancer pothole is in our lives and we must learn from it. I feel we must be changed by it; otherwise, what a waste to go through that fire, be burned, and scared but not any better. I know it's crazy to feel thankful for the cancer pothole, but I am. It happened; it was ugly and it knocked me off track. I think it was supposed to because I wasn't on the *right* track. I needed to be jolted out of my comfort zone, and received a reality check. I needed to see God had different plans for me. I was the kid who had everything planned out. *Graduate 2000. Get first real job. Get married 2001. Own a dog. Have two kids – one boy one girl, in that order and 2.5 years apart.* I needed something jolting to show me: *Thy* will be done not *my* will be done.

I don't know how longtime friends and close relatives see me. I'm not sure if the "new" Stacey seems different to them. I personally see some of my behaviors and thoughts are BC (before cancer) and some are AC (after cancer). I still get wrapped up in the hustle and bustle of the world. I lose focus and get wrapped up in nonsense at times, but I truly think it happens less often than before. I see the beauty around me and in others more than I did before. I value the time spent with a good friend and true laughter that I get to share with a few close people. I am anything but an optimist (ask Pete), but I do think we all need to take a deep breath and stay calm. We need to take a break and enjoy life more often. We need to live in a way so that people will smile when they talk about us at our funerals.

# Chapter 25: Things I want to be heard at my funeral....

1. "Ha, ha, ha, remember (laugh) the time (chortle)…"
2. "It's so hard to think of just one awesome memory of Stacey."
3. "Stacey had a great smile."
4. "How did she always look so young?"
5. "Did she ever tell you of the time she…."
6. "I loved her so much."
7. "What?! When did that happen? How much was bail?"
8. "Yeah, I remember and then the curtain started on fire, the possum ran across Edith's lap, and…."
9. "Whatever possessed her to climb out on the fire escape anyway?"
10. "She did what?"
11. "I am going to miss her."
12. "Stacey would really enjoy this mimosa!"
13. "Only Stacey would have a Chinese buffet at her funeral, and I love it!"
14. "She had so many good ideas!"
15. "Beautiful, inside and out."
16. "She could totally pull off wearing a hat!"
17. "Which adventure did she take you on?"
18. "The only bad thing I could say about the old gal is that she never got the hang of making those darn cereal bars. You know the ones."
19. "She looks *gooood*."
20. "She taught me so much."
21. "I don't even look that good today and she has been dead a week!"
22. "Is that a conga line?"
23. "I will remember her hugs."
24. "She always made me feel better."
25. "But what about after she got that third beer in her… am I right?"
26. "I will miss her every day of my life."

27. "She was a great sister, (unfortunately due to the Monarchy effect I may beat some of you to the grave). You can also insert friend, mother, aunt.
28. "Is that goat wearing a hat?"
29. "She made me feel loved."
30. "Can I get a Mello Yello?"
31. "I love the song selection." (Trust me it will be epic!)
32. "I'm so glad I told her how amazing she was."
33. "I hope I can find my ornery side, too."
34. "She *really* did make a difference."
35. "Sitting with her brought me comfort."
36. "Faith, your mom loved you so much."
37. "I never understood how she could be cold when it was 80 degrees?"
38. "She would always cry in church." "Don't forget parades, the sound of a siren, oh and in any loud crowd filled area."
39. "She prepared her daughter well for life."
40. "I loved her analogies."
41. "She made the best Lemonade Pie!"
42. "She was funny."
43. "Even our dog liked her."
44. "One of the kindest people I knew."
45. "Classy!"
46. "She tried everything."
47. "When will we know if she wins the Nobel Peace Prize?"
48. "Lovely!"
49. "She smelled so good."
50. "Her hands tell us so many stories."
51. "Her books were fantastic!"
52. "She understood me."
53. "She always made time for me."
54. "She never did like mornings."
55. "I loved her energy."
56. "How did she always get so much done?"

57. "Man, was she feisty!"
58. "Faith, your mom would be proud."
59. "I loved her cooking."
60. "I am glad she learned to love herself."
61. "Wow, what a lady!"
62. "She survived so much."
63. "Who is going to take the goat?"

## Chapter 26:  Homage to the Caregivers

According to the Merriam-Webster dictionary, a caregiver is: a person who provides direct care (as for children, elderly people, or the chronically ill). I cannot deny the proof of the definition; I just think it falls short of reality.

A caregiver is the compassionate person who will never have the physical scars the patient endures, but will share in the emotional ones. The caregiver will never physically share the same pains, soreness, and reactions to the medicine as the patient, but they will have very physical reactions to their loved one's pain. The caregiver will lose sleep thinking about what needs to be done, about the bills that are accruing, and about the outcome of all these struggles. The caregiver will shed many tears. The tears will be from fear, anger, sadness and from complete exhaustion. To make it as simple as saying it is "someone who provides direct care" is frankly, in my opinion, lame. No offense to the writers of the dictionary.

The caregivers are the ones who make it possible for the patients to go on and to have the strength to keep doing what is needed for survival. The caregivers are the people who step in and clean the bathroom when the patient has no strength to come up with a to-do list. They bring suppers, mow lawns, run errands and bring your kids to school because they know it will help. They say nothing, yet they hold a hand and they fight battles without the patient ever knowing.

I do not know what it is like to live with a cancer patient. I hope I never do. I just know when you are a cancer patient; life is made easier with the love, support, understanding compassion and duty of your caregivers.

Most caregivers are consumed in this struggle and don't realize they also will need some help. They are victims in this fight, too. In chapter twelve, I gave a list of things that are great to give to a caregiver who is too busy taking care of their loved one. I know I am speaking from the view of a cancer patient, but the truth is any caregiver, whether they are caring for a child or adult, if they are helping an Alzheimer patient or someone who has suffered a stroke or had a major accident, can use the love, support, and ideas I compiled.

The caregiver will need special attention as well. When dealing with caregivers be patient, forgiving, generous of your time, and remember they need just as many prayers as the patient. According to an article in *All You* magazine (April 2015), forty-eight percent of caregivers will continue to work while providing care for their loved ones. That usually means they haven't taken anything off their plate; they have only added more to it. Caregivers tend to just keep giving, sometimes up to the point where they are overwhelmed. The same article also said caregivers have twenty-three percent higher levels of stress hormones than that of a non-caregiver. Caregivers need to make sure they are allowing people to help them. Even if it is letting someone pick up the dry cleaning or run a child to practice, it really will help and allow them to take a breath. It will be hard, but as a caregiver please try to eat healthy, get rest, and get some exercise. You can't help the patient if you are lying in your own bed sick from the stress and lack of care you have shown yourself.
When I talk with caregivers they all say the same thing.
1. They hurt from watching their loved one suffer.
2. They are frustrated by helplessness and the fact that time is moving at a snail's pace.
3. They just want to scream because they are overwhelmed.

As I write that, I think of a PBS TV show I used to watch called *The Red Green Show*. Red's tag line after his heart-to-heart talk was, *"Remember, I'm pulling for ya; we are all in this together.*" To feel overwhelmed is natural and inevitable, but I think if we remember we are all in this together, the struggle is at least bearable.

It is a challenge when the times get tough to be patient and speak kindly. I encourage everyone to try to hold their tongues, assume the best of everyone's intentions, and use each other's skills to lighten the load. No one can or should do everything. Let multiple caregivers assign jobs instead of assigning blame.

If you are the caregiver who will be staying close to the patient and possibly not working outside the home, I would suggest keeping a binder close by so you can keep everyone informed. This communication tool will include a calendar with doctor appointments, a sign up for who is taking care of transportation and meals, and another area for medications. This can note what medication and dosages are being taken and a chart to mark when they have been given. Make a list of phone numbers and contact names. Lastly, some blank pages that allow caregivers to leave each other notes. Example: "A.M. visit today. Mom was in good spirits, color was back in her cheeks. She took her medication and I refilled her water." This will be a great place to include any details the medical staff has shared with you.

When caregivers go to appointments it is hard to remember everything that is said. It can turn into a bad game of telephone when you start to recount the details with others. Take notes and be sure to put this information into the binder.

I'd also like to suggest purchasing a large desk calendar, so everyone can have a central area to meet and gather important dates or use a shared calendar on your phone or computer. The calendar is also great to allow everyone to see when meals are being brought. Shared responsibilities can be color-coded and will allow everyone the chance to claim the jobs with which they feel comfortable.

This type of caregiver is also in charge of the atmosphere of the home for the patient. Personally, I would need this person to do their best to create the right healing space. Consideration of noise, scents, temperature etc. is essential along with the following list:

1. Change the sheets when the patient is in the shower and pull back one corner. This is welcoming when it is time to relax again.
2. When providing a cool drink for the patient, include a straw.
3. Soft music is usually a winner.
4. Having a comfy throw blanket nearby is soothing.
5. Please open the shades, possibly the windows, especially if going outside is not an option yet.
6. Encourage some kind of social time.
7. Sitting outside is healing.
8. Promote positive thoughts.
9. Silence is okay.
10. General statements and updates of the world are much better than asking the patient questions.
11. If you ask a question, maybe it could be something like, "Supper is going to be at six, are you in the mood for tortilla soup or hamburgers?" As the patient, I hate having too many options, but I can handle choosing between two. Another example is, "Church is at 8:00 or 11:00. What time should I come get you?"
12. Cards, games, and puzzles are great options to have close.
13. Magazines or books offer simple time fillers. Simple reading is my recommendation as I found it hard to concentrate.
14. Hugs are free.
15. Remember children have special healing powers; let them make short visit.
16. Taking photos during treatment is very personal, but I'd encourage it only if the patient is okay with it.

17. Be observant of routines.
18. A bowl of hard candy is a nice touch.

If you are the caregiver who fits the description of many where you are still putting in a full workday, you can remember this list as well.
1. Breathe.
2. De-stress as much as you can before you return to help the patient.
3. Set the phone aside upon entering the home.
4. Engage the patient before going into fix-it mode.
5. Caution: hold off on complaints.
6. Prioritize your to-do list.
7. Crockpot meals really do save the day!
8. If there is a sibling or spouse helping when you are not there, don't undermine or undo their efforts. Work together to make this time easier for everyone.
9. One person should be authorized to do the billing on the patient's behalf. Remember to keep everyone in the loop, though.
10. Let the extra jobs like personal errands be assigned to those who are the closest to the patient. It only makes sense; these people know the patient and will be able to give personalized care easily and without hesitation. This shouldn't be for the person who is going to stand in the deodorant aisle for 15 minutes trying to figure out if the patient is a roll on or spray kind of gal. Or if the patient would want a Powder Fresh or Paradise Escape fragrance. Send someone who can grab and go while making good choices for the patient. As I mentioned earlier these jobs are technically not important, but they do create an atmosphere that is more soothing to the patient.
11. Don't overload your plate. Cut back where you can and share the responsibilities.

I strongly suggest checking into an app called *StandWith*. This app allows caregivers to keep friends and family up-to-date about the patient without sending out numerous texts, calls, or emails. Also, it allows tasks to be fulfilled by supporters simply and quickly. Jobs like picking up the kids, giving rides to the hospitals, and pet care are just a few of the options the app allows you to personalize.

*"Alone we can do so little, together we can do so much,"*
*~Helen Keller.*

## Chapter 27. St. Peregrine

St. Peregrine was a convert to the Catholic faith in the thirteenth century. He was dedicated to his new faith and became a monk. According to Catholic.org, he observed and imposed on himself the penance to stand whenever it was not necessary to sit. When tired he would support himself on a choir stall. At the age of sixty he developed cancer in his right leg. The infection became so bad the only option was for amputation. The night before the foot would be removed Peregrine prayed he would be healed. Upon awakening his foot was healed and the doctor could find no reason to continue with the amputation. Because of his faith and dedication to God, he was healed. If you are someone who believes it is good to ask for help from someone who's been in a similar situation, you may find peace while praying to St. Peregrine through this prayer.

*Dear holy servant of God, St. Peregrine, I pray today for healing. Intercede for me!*
*God healed you of cancer and others were healed by your prayers. Please pray for the physical healing of...*
*(Mention your intentions).*

*These intentions bring me to my knees seeking your intercession for healing.*
*I am humbled by my physical limitations and ailments. I am so weak and powerless. I am completely dependent upon you God. And so, I ask that you pray for me...*

*Pray for me, that I will not let sickness bring me to despair.*
*Pray for me, that that I may persevere in hope.*
*Pray for me, that I will have the courage to offer up my suffering in unity with the Cross.*

*I know, St. Peregrine, you are a powerful intercessor because your life was completely given to God. I know that in as much as you pray for my healing, you are praying even more for my salvation. A life of holiness like yours is more important than a life free of suffering and disease. Pray for my healing, but pray even more that I might come as close to Our Lord as you are.*

*Glory be to the Father and to the Son and to the Holy Spirit. As it was in the beginning is now, and ever shall be, world without end.*

*Let me also pray that all cancer patients, as well as others dealing with chronic and life-threatening diseases, will be consoled. I pray they will experience the healing presence and love of our Lord, whether it be through prayer or through their interactions with others, especially through their family and friends.*

*I also want to remember in a special way to pray for all the families and friends who know someone suffering with cancer; may God console them too.*

*Through the witness of the saints, I know suffering has meaning. Many saints accepted suffering while others even asked for more of it. They did so because they were motivated by love and by a desire to join Christ in redemptive suffering, however painful and long. I pray my suffering will not rob me of joy. I pray I will persevere in hope, especially when I am feeling weak and weary.*

*Pray with me, Saint Peregrine, I will look to the cross; stay strong in my faith, and ever hopeful in God's will.*

*Lastly, I pray that all of my life will glorify God alone. I do not exist for any other reason. I pray to know my true purpose: for Him. Amen*

(This prayer has been adapted and modified from praymorenovenas.com.)

The last paragraph of the prayer reminds me of a beautiful woman with whom I shared my cancer journey. Tracy was remarkably strong in her faith. Joy seeped out of her every time we spoke. She would tell me all the time about how we are here to glorify God. Her constant prayer and constant jubilation for life and everything she encountered would literally have me standing in awe. She was an amazing person that never let cancer beat her. She earned her Wiggie, no doubt!

*"You beat cancer in how you live, why you live, and in the manner in which you live."*
*~Stuart Scott.*

That was Tracy.

## Chapter 28:  I'll Take a Mulligan.

A few years ago, while playing a "get to know you" board game, I was asked this question: If you ever wrote a book about your life what would the title be? Strangely enough that was a question I had been thinking about on my own. When the question came to me it didn't take long to share my answer with the group. I said quite confidently "I'll Take a Mulligan."

For those of you who have never been forced to watch a game of golf, this term may be coming out of left field, or in this case from the bunker. Though we know it comes from the Scottish game, the term has many differing origins. I can't get bogged down in those details, though. Let us trudge on with the confidence that the old mixed-up tale of where the term was first used will end in a Cinderella story, much like the best sports stories do.

The origin isn't important at this point. What we need to agree upon is the definition. When a golfer steps up to the tee on the first hole and hits a less-than-Jordan-Speith-worthy shot, a gracious golfing buddy will tell him to "take a mulligan." According to Play Golf America this means, "The hitting of a second ball, without penalty, on that hole." I am going to define a mulligan for the purpose of this tale as *a do-over*. I suppose it could be equivalent to the second serve in tennis. I'm sure kickers would appreciate a second chance when it comes to field goals, but these second chances are reserved for golfers and tennis players, I guess.

Now that we are clear about that, we may proceed.

The basic philosophy of getting another try at something with no real consequences seemed like a perfect answer to our board game question. As I look back on much of my life, I wish for a do-over. A chance to react differently. I am a bit of a perfectionist at times, and when I look back at my cancer journey I often think, *I should have been a better patient. I should have been a better advocate for other patients. I should have been a hero.* I am my own worst cheerleader and most difficult opponent. There is nothing I have conquered with such success and grace that anyone would write a book about me.

So, I wrote one myself.

I guess it was easier to write about myself than to have the pressure of living as the person I pressure myself to be. *That* would be a lot of work.

Writing this book has been very cathartic for me. I still look back and think I should have been better, but the fact of the matter is, I cannot go back. Oh heavens, I don't want another crack at being a cancer patient. I will settle on not being the best patient and live with those regrets versus doing it over again "correctly."

I didn't do things perfectly. I lost my temper. I cared too much about hair issues. I cared too much about what people thought. I was too hard on myself and didn't laugh enough. I lived in a guilty state because I wasn't the mom I always imagined I would be. I let a delayed baptism and not having baby photos taken within the first few weeks after birth eat away at me. They were hanging over my head as bullet points of how many times I screwed up as a mom. I have lived with many regrets and what-ifs.

So, here is another list:
1. I am alive.
2. Pete is still by my side.
3. Our daughter is the most amazing and coolest thing I ever helped to create.

In moving forward with the publishing of this book I am frequently asked why I wrote it. I, of course, am not able to narrow it down to a one-sentence answer. I find myself giving them a list, and here is part of it.

1. I hope that after reading through this book some of my mistakes will be avoided.
2. I hope a caregiver or two will take my advice and make sure they take care of themselves and let some friends help.
3. I hope some medical personnel will rethink their profession and get out before they become the villain in someone else's book, or maybe they will decide to strive to become the super hero for someone.
4. It would be great if the medical field would stop using nonsense statements like "it could be a minor abrasion or we may have to amputate."
5. I hope one-day gynecological offices could decorate with something besides larger-than-life framed flowers that are zoomed into the middle to expose the most private parts of the plant. I mean it is bordering on botanical pornography. Honestly, anything is better than the flowers! If it were me, I'd go with landscapes.
6. Oh, I wrote this book in hopes that the term *Ta-da!* catches on.
7. I hope as a cancer patient you have smiled at least once and made a bond with me that proves we all have some human connections.
8. I hope when you read this you thought, "Yes, that is what I have been trying to say!"
9. I pray your day two, three, or four could be made a little less ugly because of something I said.

I have always wanted a reason for why this all happened. I wanted to know cancer had happened for a reason and I wanted something good to come from it. As it stands right now, much of life returned to the way it was B.C. People have forgotten I made it through a hellish experience and lived to tell about it. Sometimes people see me now and misjudge me, not realizing I know a thing or two about being scared, alone, miserable, and weak. I also know something about being brave, incredibly happy, and the strongest person in the room. Cancer can take a lot away, but I want to focus on what it can give, too.

Cancer, whether you are experiencing it yourself or as a bystander, takes away your innocence; however, it also gives you insight that can make life seem clearer. It can give you the answers you have been longing for your whole life and make you ask many more. Cancer can give you the kick in the pants you need to say what is needed. Cancer can provide the confidence to try a new adventure, or the calm that lets you know you overreact to most things that come your way. Cancer has shown me to use my orneriness to get respect and not be thrown to the side; I don't deserve that.

Having cancer or walking next to someone who has had it has probably given you your own list of things, and I would love to hear about it. In reading the popular book *Everybody's Got Something,* by Robin Roberts, I found many quotes that really yanked me up by my bootstraps and helped me to forge forward. *"Life provides losses and heartbreak for all of us, but the greatest tragedy is to have the experience and miss the meaning."* This is something I think about a lot. Cancer is hell here on earth. I pray I learned every lesson I was supposed to because I do *not* want to repeat that class. When I was in junior high, or what people call middle school these days, we had a local weatherman come to talk to us about peer pressure and some bad choices he himself had made. I don't know why this just wasn't a reprieve from classes for me, but I can actually still remember a quote from this local television celebrity. He said *there are too many mistakes to make in this world to make them all on your own: learn from others.* So true. Yes, we will need to learn our own individual lessons from our losses and heartbreaks, but we also need to be fully aware of the lessons others have already learned.

Another quote I have found myself using from Robin is, *"Make your mess your message."* So simple. We all have a story to tell; we just need to find our words and audience to make the message heard. Ask any good cook and they will tell you the kitchen needs to get a little messy if you are going to get anything great done. The world around you is going to get a little messy, but great things are being done in and around you. Casting Crowns has a great song called "Just be Held," and the line I love is, *"Your world's not falling apart, it is falling into place."* We are reminded we aren't alone and God's got this. He will carry us and fight this fight with us. We need to trust in Him.

It may be extremely hard for you to see right now, but there is a reason for all this. I yearned for there to be a reason. An apparent reason *right that moment!* It took many years for me to see there were many reasons for cancer to rear its ugly face in my life.

1. Cancer forced me to slow down. Calming down, moving, and thinking with less fury was a true blessing. At times, I feel the insanity and need to be reminded of this beautiful lesson. Moving in a purposeful way slowly allows me to get more done than frantically trying to bilocate.

2. Cancer helped me to grow up. I started to see life and problems differently. I saw people's pain and tried to truly be there for them, offering them silence and understanding. I've learned to shake off more things, not everything, but more than I used to.

3. Cancer showed me how fragile I am. I changed from thinking nothing could take me down to knowing everything could. God has me, though, and will carry me through the tough times.
4. Cancer proved to me how strong I am. If I can make it through cancer then the chaos of a healthy life is definitely in my wheelhouse. *Roar!*
5. Cancer reiterated to me that I still had a job to do. There is such a thing as cancer guilt, I felt it. I would sit with women at conferences or fundraising events and hear their stories. I would be reminded how fortunate I was to be diagnosed early and never have a reoccurrence. Ovarian cancer is not usually found early and rarely in pregnant women. There had to be a reason I was saved. God what do you want from me? I am still not sure, but I am here on Earth for a reason.
6. Cancer gave me a voice. After shock took my voice away, I found it and started to get ornery for all future women. I started to spread the word on Facebook, to my daughter's school, to neighbors and friends who had only known the healthy Stacey.
7. Cancer transformed me into a better person. I now send those letters, make those phone calls, and stop by to visit those who are on my mind and heart. I do live a Christian life of showing mercy, love, and commitment. By no means am I where I want to be, but I am growing and getting better.
8. Cancer changed the people around me. My diagnosis tested everyone who knew me. It changed how we looked at each other and how we spent our moments together. Change is not always bad; it may just take time to adjust.
9. Cancer taught me love. Cancer brought great people into my life and opened my eyes to the people who had been there all along. I am loved and need to share love with

others around me. I need to be God's tool to show love, support, and kindness.

10. Cancer gave me my mulligan. Cancer lets you start over. It lets you reboot and take another route. Decide where you took that wrong turn, recalculate, and just go. Go where God intended you to be.

*Philippians 4:13*

*"I can do all things through Christ
who strengthens me."*

Made in the USA
Columbia, SC
02 April 2018